Raves About This Book

You know, dear, when you said you were going to quit your job and write a book, I thought you were kidding. Now, how am I going to pay the mortgage?

- Linda Myers

Holy cow, Dad. I didn't know you had 200 pages of material to say about anything!

- Rebecca Myers

Amazing! Filled with practical insight and hilarious stories. A must-read addition to your library.

- The author

A juxtapositional oeuvre superfluous to the genre.

- What William F. Buckley, Jr. might have said if he had read the book.

Filled with many words. Lots and lots of them. There are a whole lot of words here. In other words, there were far too many to actually read.

- What George W. Bush might have said if he had thought about reading the book.

Brilliant! Dilbert meets Stephen Covey.

- OK, that was me, the author again.

Design, Code, Test, Repeat:

Your Instruction Manual for a Great Software Career

By

Bill Myers

ISBN 0-7414-5013-5

Published by:

INFINITY
PUBLISHING.COM

1094 New DeHaven Street, Suite 100
West Conshohocken, PA 19428-2713
Info@buybooksontheweb.com
www.buybooksontheweb.com
Toll-free (877) BUY BOOK
Local Phone (610) 941-9999
Fax (610) 941-9959

Printed in the United States of America

Printed on Recycled Paper

Published March 2010

For Linda who encouraged me to get creative.

And for Rebecca.

Contents

What are They Paying You for Anyway? 49

Chapter 1: Why are We Here? – The Introduction

Then I'm gonna have to write a chorus,
We're gonna need to have a chorus.

- The chorus to "Happy With What You Have To Be Happy With" by King Crimson.

Can't I Just Write Code?

Your career in software is about more than just what you do for eight or more hours a day, five or more days a week. It's about the path that your career and your life take for the next 10 to 40 years. Will you climb the management ladder? Will you try to become the Chief Technical Officer at your company? Will you become a technical lead for your group? Are you content with being a valuable team player, but not in a leadership role? All of these are valuable members of the software community, but they each have different responsibilities and associated rewards. Deciding what you want to do, where you fit in, and what kind of place you want to work is up to you. You can let it choose you, or choose it yourself.

This book is about these options, but also about how to take control and how to improve your lot in the world of software. To do this you need to know many things – how to write code well is just part of it.

In order to have a great career in software, you need to:

- have technical competence.

- know who the players are in the world of software development.

- find a company that you want to work for that fits you.

- develop personal best practices that help you stand out, but that contribute to the team as well.

1

- use professional best practices that help you create and maintain your software.

- understand the role of marketing and sales in the success of your software.

- know what kinds of benefits are available to you.

- know what options are available to you in your career.

- decide what you want as opposed to what you're given.

- communicate well.

No matter what role you want to play, these things will help you improve your career. This book is one tool to help you, but there are many other tools as well. I hope to give you a jumping off point.

Bill, Why Are You Writing This Book?

First, let me say that this book has gone through several incarnations. At first it was more like a memoir, but with stories that related to the best and worst of what I've done and seen in the software field. As time went by and I got more feedback, the book has evolved into a career guide. There are still lots of stories, pictures (many friends and family have commented that the comics are a welcome addition), and lessons. However, there is a more coherent feel to the whole thing.

Now to the "Why?" It occurred to me that, although I've read many books on specific technologies and a few on how to write code better, I've yet to find a good book on how to have a good career in the software field. As mentioned earlier, it's not just about writing good code. There are lots of other things that contribute to your career. So, this book is a collection of everything I could think of that would help someone have a good career or improve their existing one.

This book is about the things that you face in a software company and the software world. Many of these are things you face in any company. I've seen fortunes within grasp lost due to overestimation, hubris, and ignoring expert opinions. I've seen successes from building award-winning software to million dollar deals. You can't buy experiences like this. Although I have my doubts, like the cop who killed someone while driving drunk after he's probably seen it happen a dozen times in his career and ought to know better said, "I hope others can learn from my experiences." Don't even get me started on Paris Hilton.

This book is a mix of anecdotes, short stories, and opinions. I owe them to a lot of people, both good and bad, at the companies that I've worked for. Some of them may recognize themselves, some may not. All of the names of people and companies still in existence have been changed to protect the innocent. All of these stories are true – to the best of my knowledge and memory.

Ask Your Doctor if This Book is Right for You

OK, you don't need to ask your doctor that. I'll tell you all you need to know right here. If you're just starting out in the software industry, this will give you an idea of what to expect. You'll find out who's who and what they do or should do and what they do and shouldn't do. If you're already experienced, you'll want to read this book to see what you might learn from me and my experiences. If you don't give a hoot about software at all, you'll get more laughs from this book than your average sitcom or comedy film. If you're a manager or other player in the industry, you'll learn about the mind of software engineers and others in your field. All of you will learn about things like software processes, best practices, and what working for different kinds of companies is like.

Side effects of reading this may include: taking a job at a company you might not have considered before, being promoted to a lead position, turning down a management position to stay in development, or pursuing a career in marketing or sales. Some of the negative side effects are the same as the positive ones mentioned above. You don't really want to know what the other possible side-effects of reading this book are, do you? I didn't think so. Some things are better left alone.

This is Organized?

This book has a rough organization to it. I've divided the chapters into the following sections:

- Hunting And Gathering – this is about job hunting, resumes, interviewing and different companies.

- What Are They Paying You For Anyway? – this is about benefits, human resources, and ethics. It starts out with a chapter about the biggest bungles I've seen in my career. You'll wonder why these people got paid at all.

- Can't I Just Wear Cologne? – this section is about the people you work with in the software industry. There are stories about marketing, sales, software, QA, and documentation people.

- What Did You Say, Scotty? – this section talks about the technical stuff like processes and best practices for software development.

- In The End – this final section talks about career options and my advice on having a great career.

You can read this in order or skip around. There are some references to people and companies that will make more sense if you read it in order, but it won't matter that much.

And a Big Round of Applause to…

There are many people to thank for helping me with this book. Since my time limit at the Oscars (the movie about this book comes out in 2020) will be only 45 seconds, I'd better do most of the work here.

First, thanks to my family. My wife, Linda, and daughter, Rebecca, give me so much on a daily basis. They've also been supportive over the years with my job situations. Finally, my wife read the book several times and listened to me blather about ideas and issues in it for months. A big thanks to my mother, Dottie Miller, who read lots of drafts and has been a big supporter of this project. My friend and former colleague Daniel Loewus read numerous drafts and told me what was boring and what he found amusing. Many thanks to other family and friends who gave me corrections and feedback.

Finally, a big high five to all of my former colleagues and companies who gave me all of the experiences that I'm now able to relate to you in this book. I was surprised at the wealth of material that I had once I started jotting down notes.

Can I Get a Section 8?

The sections in the book are all titled with something related to the topic at hand, but don't really help with locating a particular topic. The index has more descriptive topics that you can search for in the text.

What About Bob?

As you read this book, you'll notice that many of the stories are about Bob. Bob doesn't really exist, but is a character I've created to embody my experiences and that of my colleagues. Although Bob is fictional, the stories are true and most of them aren't even exaggerated.

Hunting and Gathering

This section of the book talks about resumes, interviewing, and companies. These are components of job hunting, but not the only ones. There are numerous good books on job hunting. I still like *What Color is Your Parachute*, by Richard Bolles, which presents this topic in its entirety in a practical fashion. Here, I present some key points based on personal experiences.

Chapter 2: Your Life in One or Two Pages – Resumes

Well, all the parts are there.

- My economics professor in college when he looked at my resume.

I really hate resumes, but they are a fact of life in the working world. They're part marketing, part fact, and sometimes part fabrication. I recommend sticking with the first two and leaving out the third. It may or may not pay in the long run to fabricate parts of your resume, but it's still unethical. Besides, if you do a good job with the marketing and the facts, you'll hopefully get a chance to explain what you might have had a desire to fabricate.

This will not be an exhaustive review on resume writing, just some pointers that might help you. For more extensive help, grab a book that's devoted to this topic.

My God, What Have You Done?

The most important thing you can elaborate on in your resume is your relevant experience. When I was interviewing people to work on my team, I would look to see what kinds of things people had actually done. Following are some of the things I looked for on resumes.

Objectives are mostly useless. A cover letter usually tells what is relevant to the job you're applying for. Removing the objective also gives you a few more lines you can use to add real information about your experience. Most objectives are so vague anyway, that unless you're changing your career entirely, or your focus, you're not adding anything by saying, "Seeking to apply my skills and enthusiasm in the wide range of programming needed by top companies, blah blah blah."

Do you have experience with some relevant tools that we use? It doesn't matter nearly as much if you have used a particular source control system, just that you know what it was and have used one at all. Are you familiar with bug-tracking systems? Have you touched an integrated development environment or just used an editor and makefiles?

Were you more involved with research than doing production work at previous jobs? If you've been doing research and want a job writing code, then you'd better say so. Otherwise, your resume will likely end up quickly tossed into the reject pile. Alternatively, you can modify your resume to emphasize the practical aspects of your research. This could be one of the few instances where your objective might give a hint as to a switch in your career path.

Managers do like to know where you were educated, but unless you're just out of school, they don't really care about your GPA or what your Master's thesis topic was unless it's particularly relevant to the job you're applying for.

Tell about what you've done in previous jobs. This is really where the marketing aspect comes in. You've only got a few lines to sell someone on the fact that you *rock* as a developer or prospective developer. Sure, you can add action words like initiated, spearheaded, integrated, developed, enhanced, etc., but make sure you add some meat, please. Employers want to know that you actually did some work and what it involved. Are you a key person on your team or just a role player? Either one is fine, but they may be looking for one as opposed to the other. Over-marketing yourself can be a detriment as well. When a hiring manager talks to you on the phone, they'll be able to tell fairly soon that you're over-selling yourself in your resume. At the same time, countless people under-sell themselves on resumes.

Interests are useless and should be saved for personal conversation with a hiring manager. Use the room on your resume for more description of work you've done.

Nothing on a resume is more useless than "References available upon request." Duh. Have you ever heard anyone say, "I see that you don't have the phrase 'References available upon request' on your resume. Does that mean that you don't have any?" Of course not.

All the Parts are There

First of all, forget perfection. Perfection on a resume is impossible. You want good grammar and spelling, but that's a given. For everyone who likes your resume in the format you have it in, there will be a person who'd like it in a different format.

While it's important to have a "complete" resume, there's a lot more to it than just having all the right parts.

Perfection and parts aside, there are certainly resumes that are so far from perfection that they shouldn't be sent out. At Rocky International, Tim had such a resume. He had been out of college for two years and was very good at what he did, but his resume was terrible. It had the wrong year of graduation and incorrect dates of employment. I read it and thought he'd only been working for six months instead of two years. His description of what he did was taken from a job description rather than an account of what he'd actually done. It said things like, "Will implement software according to established standards in accordance with dictated requirements." He might have changed the tense of the sentence, but does that tell you anything at all? We sat down for a while and worked on it to come up with something that wouldn't end up in a trashcan — at least not immediately.

I've received resumes across the spectrum from spare to excessive. Some resumes look like the person threw it together in an hour and doesn't think that much of himself. If that's the case, the person reading it won't think too much of you either.

When you send out your resume, you want to accomplish two things. First, you want it to say that you're competent and capable. Second, you want it to get you an interview so you can sell yourself in person. Tell about the best stuff you've done and leave out the rest unless it's relevant to the job or rounds out your experience. Don't go over the top on style and flair. A clean, easy to read format that lets someone get a sense of you quickly is best. One resume I received a long time ago had a picture of the American Eagle from the back of a one dollar bill on it. The resume was actually very good, but I got the immediate impression that this guy thought a little bit too much of himself.

Have a couple of people look over your resume and ask them to critique it honestly. If you can't seem to get it right yourself, then you might go ahead and have a professional help you. If you do, make sure that they're helping you with the content and not just making it prettier and printing copies for you on nice paper. Prices for this start at around $100, but can go to over $500!

Just the Facts, Ma'am

Every once in a while, someone gets the idea that they should get really creative with their resume. I remember reading a story about this and some of these resumes were truly interesting, but ultimately ineffective. My favorite story was that a guy received a resume that was written in C code. He promptly compiled the code and sent the compiler error and warning output back to the candidate. I don't think he got the job.

Creativity has a place, but unfortunately, it needs to stay within the bounds of what is considered standard practice. If you want to get creative, think of a great way to paint your experiences in words on your resume. Leave it at that.

And Now for the Main Course

So far, we have talked about some of the things to include and not include in general. When someone who is hiring reads a resume, they will likely fall into one of two categories. The first type of hiring manager is looking for someone that he can plug into a current position and will hit the ground running. Their group writes C++ code on Windows and they want you to have that experience. Naturally, if you have this kind of experience, it should be obvious on your resume because you've listed it in your technology or skills section. If you don't have this kind of experience, this potential employer is unlikely to give you a second thought. However, the second type of hiring manager is looking for someone who *can* write C++ on Windows, but may be willing to accommodate someone who hasn't yet. They may be willing to train you, especially if they feel you'll bring some other valuable experience to their team. Moving from Java to C++ isn't exactly a breeze, but it's certainly doable. Both languages involve object-oriented programming skills, so you should highlight that particular skill on your resume. Remember that technologies may come and go, but your ability to learn new technologies, apply skills, and adapt to new situations is a constant. You need to tell potential employers about that.

If you have been working for a while, you know what you've done and what you can do. When you describe your job, you need to put it into words that tell potential employers that you are a genius who needs to be put to work in their office. Tell them how you've mentored new employees in your field of expertise. Be sure to note that you're now the technical lead on some aspect of a project or product. Tell what you have actually accomplished. For example: "I lead my group of three engineers through the first release of the sub-atomic graphical model generator software. We received a commendation on our outstanding performance on the project," sounds better than: "Worked on sub-atomic graphical model generator." The former relates leadership abilities and also implies that since it was a first release, you helped to take something up from the ground floor.

If you are about to graduate or have recently graduated from college and have limited work experience, you have a much more difficult job. An employer looking for someone to hire in an entry-level position needs to know that you're smart and will be able to learn and contribute quickly. Of course, you'll need time to ramp up your skills – they know that – but, they don't want to wait 6 months before you can write a single line of useful code. Most resumes from college students look the same. They list classes they have taken, their GPA, and a few technologies they've learned in school. How can you make your resume tell a potential employer that they should interview you?

First of all, tell what you've done. You can enhance this by actually doing more than your fellow students. If you can find a co-op program or take a summer job doing programming, then you have a leg up already. Either way, in addition to the courses you have taken, tell what you *did* in a few of them. I'm not saying that your resume should read: "In C++ class we learned about pointers, arrays, characters, classes, etc." I am saying that if you did a project that took you two weeks to complete (and not just because you were clueless for 13 days) then tell about it like it was a job accomplishment. For example, "Working in a group with two other students, we designed and coded a working GPS locator to find the nearest coffee shop that isn't a Starbucks. The application ran on a standard GPS-enabled cell phone. We also demonstrated how this could be used for other practical applications by using several interchangeable interfaces. We were commended for creating the most innovative and elegant solution the professor had ever seen." All of a sudden, it seems like you really did something that might be attractive to employers, doesn't it?

In the end, your resume needs to describe what you have done and that it conveys what you can and will do for your future employers.

Lost in Translation

One final note about resumes. They should be in plain English (assuming that you live in an English-speaking country). Nothing funky, hip, gnarly or whatever slang is current when you read this book. You must envision who's likely to be reading it.

The simple truth is that you have no idea who'll be reading it. Stick to simple and straightforward.

Discussion and Thought Questions

1. If you were a hiring manager reading your resume, would you want to talk to this person? If not, get some help improving it.

2. Have you had a couple of other people give you feedback on your resume?

Chapter 3: How to suck and how not to – Interviewing

I know he can get the job, but can he do the job?

> - Joe's boss in "Joe vs. The Volcano"

He can be taught!

> - The genie in "Alladin"

Before you can have a great career in software (or any field for that matter) you have to land the job. If you're a student coming out of school, it's likely, but not strictly true, that most of your experience is academic. In interviewing students, it is the ones who can talk about real projects that they worked on that stand out. If you have an opportunity to do an internship or co-op program, by all means take it. The practical experience you get and the connections you can make will be invaluable. You'll also have the opportunity to find out which fields of software and particular tasks you like and which ones you dislike.

Even if you've been working for a while, you can still have lousy experiences in interviews. Unfortunately, every time you have to interview for a job, it has likely been a few years since the previous time. Like any other skill, interviewing is one that improves with practice and your first one or more are likely to be a bit rocky.

In addition to being interviewed, you'll have to interview other people as well. This gives you other opportunities to suck or not to suck. Making a bad call has long-lasting and painful consequences. Making a good call can really improve your team and your own performance and image.

How to Suck at Being Interviewed

We'll start out with a few instructive cases where interviewing did not go very well. If you can't learn from your mistakes, you're doomed to keep repeating them. Hopefully, you can learn from these before you make similar ones.

I'll Take Door Number Four, Monty

It was 1986 and Bob was on his way to an interview in Boston with a company called ICON. I don't know what you know about driving in Boston, but take this advice – if you have to drive in Boston, don't. At least not without a great map that shows all of the one-way streets, a good navigator, and lots of extra time. Boston is a small big city. It's not huge, but it is a major city nonetheless. One way that it stays even reasonably manageable is that back in the 1700s, the city planners got together and decided that the streets should be laid out in a pattern that's vaguely reminiscent of a tornado. If you try to do the reasonable thing and drive along a path that will take you in the general direction you want to go, you'll be ejected from the city – dumped out on the other side as if you're simply not worthy of being there. I suspect that they assumed this would keep out the riff-raff.

This is how Bob came to be two hours late for his interview. He had neither a good map, nor a good navigator, and was armed only with directions that even Bostonians couldn't understand. For example, they could all tell you where the Pepper Pot Bridge is, but not its official name, the Longfellow Bridge. Thus, his day did not begin well.

Before we proceed, a little background on people coming out of graduate school or college as Bob was. People coming out of school don't know anything about the working world (some would say that even experienced people only know what life is like at their previous companies and their potential new one is going to be different enough that they might as well know nothing). If you're a graduating student, you probably do know some things. You probably know a lot about the project that you're working on for your thesis if you're a graduate student. You probably have a lot of book knowledge and maybe some practical knowledge about some of your field, but don't think that you really know what's going on. What you know is mostly academic. Some of it is indeed transferable to the working world, but you have much to learn. Here's the big thing, though, and get this through your head as quickly as possible. YOU DON'T KNOW JACK. If you're anything like most students (I was like this, too), you get the sense that you're smarter than everyone else (sorry, you're not). This makes you talk down to people and overestimate yourself. I've found that even seasoned professionals can have similar traits in this respect. Now back to the interview. First, Bob met with the development group.

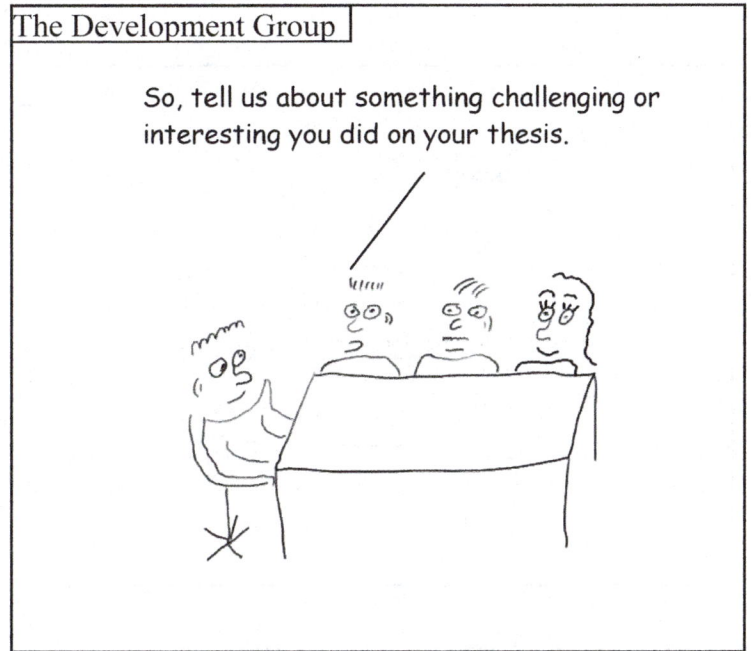

Later on, he realized that what he thought was so clever was old hat to developers who write code every day.

The application group didn't even go *that* well.

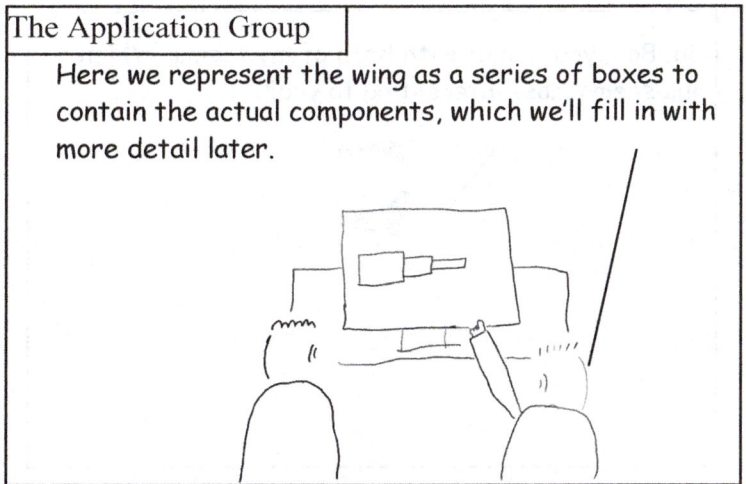

Bob was a bit confused, due to a less than perfect explanation and poor listening skills, so he thought it best to ask a question.

Of course, you're stunned that *anyone* would say something so stupid in an interview, but thus goes the hubris of the graduating student. Then, things went further downhill for Bob when he met with the company President, Barry Rose.

So, Bob, you've met with both of my teams. Which one seems most interesting to you?

Well, neither group, really. I'd really like to work on a library of things that fits in between the two groups.

I guess we don't really have a good fit then.

No, I guess not.

For future reference, if a guy asks you to choose between two options and picking one of the two gives you a shot at a job, pick one. Picking an option that's not on the table is not a good idea.

If you don't see yourself in this description, good for you. Now look harder. Not a trace? Really? Good, then you'll have a better day than Bob did. If Bob had gotten this job, he would have moved to Boston. Instead of the career and life he has now he might still be trying to find his way to work. If he was deemed worthy of staying in Boston, of course.

Springs and Things

Bob went on another interview that didn't go very well, but in a different way. His problem this time was more due to his inability to read people well. He had an interview with the now defunct Digital Equipment Corporation. One of his graduate school colleagues had already been working in this group for a year and seemed to be enjoying himself well enough. Bob felt that he had a good shot at a job. He talked with numerous people and then ran into the two tough guys. The first one asked for a technical proof of an engineering equation. Although he got off to a good start, he couldn't think of the secret sauce to add to make it work out and had to admit defeat.

Then things got worse when he met with the hiring manager.

Well, I'm sure you saw this coming, but he really did talk himself out of the job. Moral - don't argue about the small stuff. If the interviewer is convinced of something, it doesn't pay to argue on principle. He would have been happy doing the job and would have eventually found out who was right.

Could You Repeat That a Few More Times

OK, nobody really gets tied up and interrogated under hot lights during a job interview, but sometimes they can feel like that. After a couple of years working for Ram Technology, Bob saw the writing on the wall. The main company, the Maclean Corporation, was letting his division, Ram Technology, go downhill and didn't seem to care too much about it. He started looking around and found out that a major company in his field, ABDC, was looking for a *lot* of people. He sent a resume to them and got a call one night from a hiring manager, Vikram. They had a great conversation. The job sounded interesting, the work was right up his alley, and Vikram seemed interested in Bob. Later that same evening, another hiring manager, Vijay, from another group at the same company called. They had a nice conversation, too, but he couldn't believe that Bob would actually be interested in the other group that he had just talked to. At that time in his career and in his life, he wasn't terribly picky. That's not to say that he would have taken a job that he would have hated, but as long as there was good work to be done, nice people to work with, and a product that he thought was promising, he would have been happy there. Vijay even told him that they needed so many people that "Unless you totally blow it, we'll probably offer you a job." Of course, by now, you've read about his fantastic history with interviewing, so you can see where this story is going, can't you? Anyway, he made arrangements to travel to their site the next week and would interview with both teams. It was to be one hell of a day.

He flew in the night before and stayed at a hotel near the company's headquarters. The next morning, he met a guy for breakfast. He was a higher level manager and was taking a training class, so this was his only time to meet. They had a nice talk and he gave Bob the schedule for the rest of the day. Full house. He was to talk to fourteen people throughout the day. It seemed that he sure picked a bad week to stop sniffing glue. (You have to remember the first Airplane movie to catch that reference, but it conveys his feelings either way.)

If that wasn't packed enough, nothing could have prepared him for the kind of interviewing he would be subjected to. Imagine a day where you would spend 30 minutes apiece with 10 people (the other 4 are excluded from this description) who would each ask you the same three dull and unrevealing questions. Well, that's what happened. In succession he was asked:

1. "What did you do in your last job?" Unfortunately, this was why he was leaving his last job. The initial promise of some really interesting work was shoved aside and although it wasn't terrible, he worked on some tasks that really weren't all that flashy or interesting to relate in an interview. Therefore, his answer to that question wasn't great. Now the job before that one was packed with great stuff, but nobody thought to ask about that, nor did he think to simply tell them about all of the creative and interesting things he had done in all of his jobs. The key thing here was that it didn't occur to him at the time that he should try to steer the conversation. A simple question was asked and he gave them a simple answer.

2. "Why are you leaving your current job?" Well, the answer to that was the same as the answer to the first question, with the addition that the company was going downhill.

3. Bob couldn't remember the third question, actually, but it was something equally dull like: "Where do you see yourself in five years?"

Finally, he met with the two hiring managers. Vijay asked him a bunch of hypothetical questions which he didn't do well on because, well, they were hypothetical. If you want to really understand someone, ask them a specific, but open-ended question about what they've actually done, not what they *would* do. You'll get a more honest answer about someone's experience. For example, he asked how much time you should spend designing code versus writing code. Bob thought for a minute and came out with what he thought Vijay wanted to hear, namely, lots of time designing versus not so much writing. Unfortunately, that's not what he actually does, nor does he think that's the correct answer. The correct answer is much more complicated. It depends on the particular project, how well you understand it, and how well you understand the code that it has to operate with. Is it a separate bit of code or is it something that must be intertwined with lots of other code? Now if he had asked an open-ended question like, "What has been your experience in designing code?" then Bob could have told him that as well as how he thinks that developing a prototype is important sometimes, etc.

Bob and the other hiring manager, Vikram, actually sat down with the software so that he could see a demonstration. This is a great tool for interviewing, actually. The candidate gets to talk about the functionality of the software and show that he has a clue about what's going on with it. He can ask intelligent questions and tell anecdotes about his experience doing similar things. Unfortunately, if the interviewer doesn't stop and think about how this relates to what you know and how well you would work there, then it's academic.

In the end, Bob didn't get any job offers from them. After some reflection, he came to the conclusion that although he did blow it, it wasn't entirely his fault. One of the things that's hardest to do is to steer a bad interview in a better direction for you, but it's essential. It was also the fault of the fine folks at

ABDC, who could stand some work on their interviewing skills. I'll talk about that later in the chapter.

How Not to Suck at Being Interviewed

It's the Network

A couple of months after his boneheaded interview at ICON, Bob decided that his best shot at an interesting job in his particular area of interest was to go to a conference, do some networking (this was before the buzzword was coined, so he was way ahead of his time), and see what he could dig up. On the plus side, the conference he was interested in was only a 30 minute drive away in downtown Philadelphia. After a long, but interesting day, he wasn't any closer to landing a lead on a job, although he did have an impromptu interview with some guys who were doing some work related to his expertise at the time. As he was sitting on the bus heading from the convention center back to his car, he struck up a conversation with a man sitting next to him.

Good conference, long day, wouldn't you say? I'm Bob, nice to meet you.

Hi, I'm Jim. I agree, very interesting stuff going on. What brings you here?

Well, I'm just out of graduate school and I'm looking for a software job. Did you meet anyone who's looking for an engineer?

Actually, I did. I met these guys from Bainey Systems who are looking for someone just like you. Here's a business card from them.

Bob went home and made a couple of phone calls to Bainey Systems.

He landed an interview for the next week. During the interview, things were going well, but the hiring manager was having some reservations about Bob's actual engineering experience. Some of the customers who would be using the software were going to be using it for structural applications.

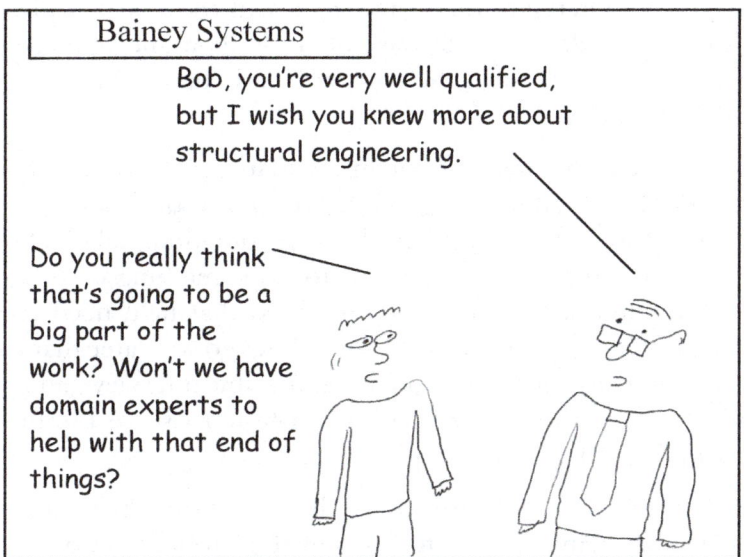

In the end, Bob was able to plant the seed in the hiring manager's mind that perhaps the domain expertise wasn't as important as the other qualifications that he had. He got the job, spent seven years working there, and didn't need to know a bit of structural engineering.

Bob did a lot of things right in finding and getting this job. He met face to face with people at a conference, struck up conversations with people, made connections, and overcame resistance to some of his shortcomings in experience during his interview.

I'll Make a Note of it

At another point in his career one of Bob's colleagues told him about a small startup that was right down the street called BDI. Since he lived in a medium-sized town (30 to 40 thousand people), high-tech companies weren't exactly a dime a dozen like they were in the Silicon Valley. Finding a company down the street from him that did similar work was an amazing stroke of luck.

He got an interview there and met with several people. It started with a demo, so he was able to look at and understand what was going on with the software, and convey some of his domain knowledge.

Later that day, he met with the hiring manager, Harry Feldman. He and Harry had a very good conversation, but then he was asked a tough test question. It was something like, "How would you structure an algorithm to do something or other?" Bob gave him a few ideas, but admitted that he'd need more than a minute to come up with something good. Later that day, Bob sent Harry a thank you note for the interview and included some more coherent ideas on how to solve the problem. In the end, he got that job, too.

Bob's example here demonstrates that it can only help to write a personal thank you note (an email is today's norm) and include something specific from the interview to drive home why you would be a great employee.

As the Boy Scouts Say...

Be Prepared! Preparing for an interview takes a little time. It's best to start a few days in advance, depending on how important the interview is and how much you really want the job. The problem, of course, is that you may not know how cool a job is going to be until the interview.

There's a lot you can do to prepare for interviews. First, you should do some research on the company. Find out what they do, what their products are, what their technology is, how their stock is doing, how big they are, etc. See if you can download their software beforehand and get to know it a bit. You'll be able to speak more intelligently about what they do. If you can't download the software, try to arrange a demonstration as early in the day as possible.

If you know that the position will involve a particular computer language, brush up on it. Look on the web for a list of commonly asked interview questions. Chances are that your interviewer may have gotten his questions from the same site. If you know what the domain of the company is, see if you can think of the underlying knowledge you'd want to have to work in the field. For example, a fellow manager at Ottobon would ask co-op candidates about vector mathematics. He figured that they had learned this in a class on linear algebra or maybe in calculus. Since we used vectors in our graphics and geometry work, this was useful knowledge to have.

One other thing that seems to pop up frequently in interviews is data structures. I've been tested on linked lists, binary searches, hash tables, and trees. It seems like basic computer science is still a required source of knowledge by some potential employers.

Interviewing Others

In my years of work, I've had the "pleasure" of interviewing others, both as a potential colleague and manager. The one sure thing is that it's a pain and a crapshoot (never mind, I know that's really two things). I'll tell you about a couple of the more colorful interviews that I've done and then a bit about how you should go about interviewing other people.

The Wanderer

While looking for a new software development manager, the Director of Engineering, Jack Callahan, decided that he would invite people to come out for two days of interviewing. The team would talk to the candidate all day, take him out to dinner, then have him back the next day for more punishment. They brought in a guy who looked like a major player for this treatment. He had run his own company, written a couple of well-known books, and some other impressive stuff. They couldn't imagine why he was interested in a first-line management position, but what the hell, what did we have to lose? Time, actually.

During the two days, they found out two very important things. One, he knew some very interesting things about writing software. Two, he was a great verbal tap-dancer.

Bob was a manager at the time and said that in his entire life, he'd never seen anyone in a job interview who could take a direct question and divert it into a ten minute rave about something else. The answer always had a shred of the initial question, but never came close to what you were looking for. He should have been in politics. After Bob talked to him one day and got nowhere, he had the opportunity to try again the second day. He finally gave Bob a strategy for one of the questions that he'd asked him the previous day about his experience with scheduling in software projects. Since he hadn't really done any, he had tap-danced the day before. This day, he said he would go out and buy the top four books on the subject and figure out how to do it. It wasn't a great answer as scheduling is both and art and science, but at least he finally said something that was on target.

Later that day, Jack was interviewing him and after listening to a few minutes of skirting the subject again, finally put his foot down and said, "Either answer my questions directly or this interview is over!" Needless to say, we didn't hire him.

The moral is: there's a line between steering an interview to your benefit and taking the exit ramp to the highway heading in the opposite direction. The line really isn't that fine.

The Philosopher

Bob was interviewing people for a position on his team and found a guy named Ivan who was about to graduate with a Ph.D. in computer science from a nearby university. In the past, they had had some very good luck hiring smart people who were lacking in some software experience and teaching them how to write software. If you have an engineering background, you've probably done a bit of programming in school anyway and the problem-solving skills are useful in both fields. This guy even had a background in computer science, so while his practical experience seemed to be lacking, he seemed promising.

They had Ivan come in for a half day of interviewing. He was polite and likeable, but clearly lacking in experience – pretty much what they expected. The problem was that for a guy who had very little practical experience, he had a philosophy about everything. He'd say things like, "My philosophy on starting a new coding project is to sit down and do some rough design work before starting a prototype." It sounds reasonable enough doesn't it? But since he'd never had a real job, it was a bit questionable. Additionally, his answers to most of the other

35

questions were just vague philosophies as well. Now this guy had been a teaching assistant for a Java class, so he should have been able to come out with something concrete based on his work on a Ph.D. in computer science, right?

Unfortunately, they didn't do a great job that day of really testing his Java coding skills. Instead, even though they had doubts, they hired him under the assumption that, like other people fresh from school, the equations:

```
Education = Brain

Brain + Mentoring = Future Valuable and
Productive Employee
```

would hold true. It didn't. The guy couldn't code his way out of a paper bag. They tried to get his feet wet by having him check some code out of the source code repository, copy and paste some changes into the files, compile and test them, then check them back in. Believe it or not, he needed help with the copying and pasting part. Not how to use copy and paste tools, but finding the same code in the other files and putting the right code in there. After giving him several mentors, having him audit another Java course, and giving him 9 months (much too generous) to get up to speed, they had to give up and let him go. He went back into academia and is a Professor somewhere now. He was indeed a smart guy, but just wasn't made for the kind of work they were doing.

In the end, if you have doubts, you're better off passing on a candidate or perhaps having a short trial period, if that's possible, to truly assess whether you have a winner on your hands. Better yet, try some of the suggestions below to remove the doubts and clarify the candidate's true potential.

Fog Lamps

Some experts have likened the interview process to a coin flip with the results of making a good decision about a candidate as just that accurate. Those are pretty bad odds considering the effort you're likely to put in and the implications of the decision.

It's clear to me that using one simple method of job interviewing alone doesn't tell you much. For example, you may use the knowledge test method. For one job interview, Bob received a test that took him several hours to complete that consisted of thought and coding questions. This was for a transfer within the company he was already working for! It's hard to imagine a bigger turnoff for someone. However, you may simply prefer to have one or two of your interviewers ask a few technical questions. If you do this (if the person interviewing claims to know a lot about that particular topic, you *should* do this) then you should mainly test the mainstream knowledge. Many people can't remember some of the fringe cases in a language because they just don't run into them very often, if at all. A safe assumption is that if you say you're a C++ programmer, you can talk about some of the language features, but don't need to be able to rewrite the compiler in the half hour interview.

One method some people advocate is the behavioral interviewing process. The idea is that you ask open-ended questions that let people tell you about their experiences and behaviors. For example, you might say, "Tell me about a situation in which you were faced with a seemingly impossible deadline. How did you handle it?" Almost everyone has faced this and will be able to tell you how they pulled a few all-nighters, negotiated a more reasonable subset of the work, negotiated a new deadline, or a combination of the three. Most of the answers that you get will be reasonable and won't send up a red flag. You may get something very creative that will signal a real talent. You may also get an answer like, "Well, deadlines at our last company were such a joke that we usually just waited a couple of days until management changed their minds." This should be probed a bit. Does this person therefore assume that every company does this? Do they treat every deadline as a joke? A follow-up question about another example from them might be appropriate to make sure that they do actually have a work ethic, but their last company left their willingness to go the extra mile in ruins. Now if your company also does this, you may be looking for someone who's always willing to work all night on your slightest whim. Please don't call me if you need another body.

You never know what someone might reveal in an interview. While interviewing a candidate for a position on a technical software team, Bob asked an open-ended question. Although not directly related to the question asked, that person said that they didn't like math very much. Bob felt that this was pretty important to some of the work that they did, so he didn't recommend him for the job. As it turned out, they hired him anyway. Things didn't work out very well for him, either. However, he has since found success writing other kinds of software.

As with the story about Ivan above, there are many kinds of software to be written and they often involve a different kind of mindset. If you're not adept at one kind or are tired of doing what you're doing, look around for another type of software development. On a personal note, after writing object-oriented software for many years, I grew tired of trying to unravel the spaghetti code that this often generates, even when written by good, smart engineers. I found a software job in a different field using a graphical programming language. It was a refreshing change of pace that offered new challenges of its own.

Many people still use the "look over the resume" method. They'll glance over the resume and pick out a few things to ask about. This is a good way to get someone to tell you about the specifics of their experience and performance. If you do this, try to get the candidate to tell you how they had to learn something new, applied some creativity, worked across teams, developed an interesting solution or algorithm, performed some research into established solutions, or worked collaboratively with their colleagues to get something done.

As mentioned before, giving a demonstration of any existing software can open many avenues of conversation so be sure to listen to and evaluate the candidate's reaction to it. It also lets the candidate talk about relevant experience, comment on something, or ask questions. Remember, when you work with this person, you probably expect that they'll be operating as part of a team. You want to be able to have a conversation with this person, describe a problem and have them help, or vice versa. How many of you have worked with a person who's impossible to communicate with? I can see your hands from here.

The ideal interviewing method is a combination of all of the above. The more contexts that you have for getting the feel for a person's previous performance, ability to communicate, ability and willingness to learn, flexibility, work ethic, creativity, and general competence, the better. Have different people do different jobs in the interview process then meet at the end of the day and have everyone briefly review what happened in their interview. If you simply ask everyone for a yea or nay, you won't get the benefits of a discussion of an issue that may have come up in the interview.

Finally, remember that the best people don't always have all of the experience you're looking for. What you want to know is - can she do the job? Can he be taught?

In the end, if you're not willing to put in some time and effort, you may as well just flip a coin.

Discussion and Thought Questions

1. Have you practiced interviewing lately? Have you brushed up on answers to commonly asked questions?

2. If you didn't get the last job you interviewed for, have you gone over the interview in your head to see where you might have done better?

3. If you're interviewing someone, do you have a strategy for doing so or are you just planning to wing it?

Chapter 4: Super-Size Me – Working for Different Sized Companies

In all large corporations, there is a pervasive fear that someone, somewhere is having fun with a computer on company time. Networks help alleviate that fear.

- John C. Dvorak

I'm a firm believer in having fun at work. I'm not saying that you should spend your days playing *World of Warcraft* instead of writing code, but that you should try to make your work fun. There are many different sizes and kinds of companies and each has its pros and cons. Here are a few examples and some hints on what to look for.

Mighty Mouse – The Small Startup

 Every startup begins with an idea or a vision. Most of them also have a dream that some day the company will be really cruising along and making money. Maybe they'll be able to go public or stay private, but challenge the Goliath of the industry. Nowadays, this is exemplified by the world of the web. Many times these companies started with a simple, but brilliant idea and it may not have been too difficult to code an initial implementation.

My experience is more with application development, which has bigger startup costs and longer development cycles, but the company sizes will likely give them similar personalities. Most startups that aren't created by just hacking up a web site in their spare time begin with a core group of people. They'll usually have a few developers, maybe a marketing or sales person, and someone who acts as the President or CEO. Money is usually tight unless they are well financed by a rich investor, possibly one of the people in the group. Nonetheless, when someone is spending their own money, they tend to do it conservatively. Benefits, described in more detail in another chapter, are usually adequate, but not exceptional.

The best part about working for a small startup is the environment. The team is usually small and you'll know everybody. Because it's small, everyone usually pitches in wherever they can. Work attire and general attitude are both very informal. People wear jeans and t-shirts instead of business casual clothing and everyone is called by their first name. There's a feeling of camaraderie and teamwork.

Since there's often a small budget, the office space is frequently given short shrift. Developers are likely to work in a "bullpen," which is just a collection of tables and chairs for people to put computers on. There may or may not be an individual desk in which to keep any personal items. The plus side of this setup is that everyone tends to know what's going on. Conversations take place freely and people join in when they overhear things. The negative side is that there's little privacy and you can't get much peace and quiet when you need to concentrate. For the record, individual offices have been shown to be more conducive to programmer productivity [Peopleware 1999].

The success rate for small startups growing up to larger companies or even surviving more than a few years is, unfortunately, quite low. You may find yourself out of a job in a short time. I was at BDI for a year when they had to find a buyer for the company. They had been around for several years as a consulting company, but when they decided to become more like a startup and create their own products, it took only two years to run the cycle.

Small companies that actually do grow larger usually get to the point where they need to go through a transition from thinking small to thinking larger. More people are needed, usually in the marketing and sales areas, and the type of leadership usually needs to change as well. It may be that the CEO, who was a technical person, needs to step aside to a lead technical position and hire a business-oriented person to keep things growing. You may find at this point that the environment of the company starts changing as well. The place may feel less personal. The new CEO or other newly hired Vice Presidents may be new to the software business. They may walk around and see that people are not at their desks in the evening and wonder why people aren't working every weekend either. They don't realize that software developers have lives outside of work, too. Additionally, many developers do a lot of their best problem-solving when they're not staring at a computer.

All in all, a small startup can be a lot of fun, if you're willing to put up with the lack of security it brings. You may end up handsomely wealthy in a few years if things go really well. However, like the temporary web millionaires in the 1990's during the dotcom boom, don't count your money until your stock or stock options are fully vested and able to be sold.

The Division

No, this is not another top-secret government agency doing covert operations. Whistler Technology, a software group within a decidedly non-software oriented company had the feel of a startup, but the financial backing of a huge corporation. While they went through some of the same things that a small company might have gone through in growing and struggling, the one thing that they had was some security. There were good benefits and nice offices, but a casual working environment.

While at Whistler, Bob had the opportunity to help start the product and "small company" from the ground up. He attended conferences and meetings in New Orleans, Seattle, Minneapolis, Los Angeles, Philadelphia, and Houston. He gave demonstrations and training classes in England, Japan, and Germany. As a young engineer who liked seeing new places, it was great fun.

At work he would write and test code, write documentation, perform builds, give training classes, and anything else that needed to be done. The amount of work variety in a small company can be a great opportunity to learn a lot about the business. When the little company was sold to its competitor, there was a feeling of personal loss amongst the entire group.

While you have the financial backing and a seemingly secure future, this will not be uniformly true. Your startup division may only have a small window in which to become profitable, say two or three years. Before taking a job, ask about these expectations. You and your leaders may be told that you have all the time in the world, but this may or may not be true. Business climates change and so does corporate health and corporate sentiment toward money pits. If your division isn't paying for itself or providing a service to the rest of the company, somebody's budget is going to have a red line on it with your division's name on it and that might spell the end for your party.

Big Momma's House

No, this isn't meant to indicate any person or company in particular; I just like the name of the movie, although I've never actually seen it. The basic idea here, though, is that life is different when you're living in a big house with people you may never meet making all of the big decisions. While this is similar to the description of the division above, life in a big software company can have a different feel than life in a software division of a non-software company.

In a large software company, everyone is in a division of some sort or another, but since you're all writing software, your independence is often more limited. At Ottobon, even though we were in a remote office, the feel of the place changed from project to project. In my first project there, we had just been hired away from BDI. We were given a new product to develop and since we were remote, we were left alone to do this. This had pros and cons. Our director was in California and came to visit frequently. She kept us insulated from some of the corporate problems, but helped with the connections we needed. At the time, the company was in great shape. The economy was good and they were making tons of money. In the main offices, they would have a happy hour every Friday afternoon with the company supplying the beer. Arrangements were made for us to do the same in New York.

It always seemed like the company was looking for ways to give money away. Several kinds of bonuses, stock options, clothing with a corporate logo or product name, and gifts were sent out regularly. After the first version of our new software was released, the company threw a major party. There was a band, cocktails, dinner, and dancing held at a nice local hotel. Life was good.

When the economy took a downhill turn, so did the perks. Salaries and raises were frozen, bonuses weren't given and reorganizations happened. Reorganizations in large companies are a constant. As a result, I have so many unused business cards it's ridiculous. I never changed jobs, but my division and its Vice President changed numerous times, and the business cards changed accordingly.

At one point, the company decided that its image was too stodgy. It was during the dotcom boom and everyone wanted to be part of the web explosion. Although we weren't a web site company selling pet food for twice the price of your local grocery store, the company wanted to convey that they were hip. Naturally, this called for a new corporate font. Yes, I mean font. So now the company formerly known as **Ottobon**, would be called ottobon (yes, the capital letter was changed to lowercase). Our business cards were reprinted and my name was no longer spelled out at the top of the card as "William L. Myers," but was now "bill.myers@ottobon.com." For the next few weeks, people would refer to each other as their new dotcom names. "Hi, Bill dot Myers," I would hear as I walked down the hall. We got a new sign in the new font outside the building, too. After the dotcom bubble burst our font changed again, Ottobon was capitalized again, and we got new business cards and corporate signs. I became "William L. Myers" again. Just call me Bill.

Since Ottobon was a big software company they had good benefits and made lots of money, but still had a kind of software feel to it. Dress was casual, the CEO was still called by his first name, and you could bring your dog to work in some offices. It was one of my favorite places to work, despite some of the crazy stories I will tell you in the pages to come.

Battlestar Galactica or Deep Space 9 or The Deathstar

The biggest company I ever worked for was also the smallest. What? Well, I really worked for a small local company called Diligent Systems that subcontracted me to a monstrous company called Rocky International. This was my first experience as a contractor and also working for a very formal, rigid defense contractor.

You Are Here

Talk about a change - I was blown away. Just to get into the parking lot you had to scan your security badge. After you walked for five minutes from the back of the parking lot, you'd scan your badge again to get into the building. Some rooms and labs had more security protection. After a couple of days, your access to the room would be approved and you could get in with your badge or maybe you'd have to punch in a pass code. On my first day, I watched videos on sexual harassment, information security, and diversity, and had to sign forms stating that I had watched, understood, and would abide by them. Access to some software was also regulated and sometimes you'd have to wait several days to get into a database that you needed. At the end of every day, you had to clean off your desk of all work-related papers and lock them up. Before you left the building, you'd go and check the desk of the person who left before you (there was a check-off sheet on the wall) and make sure their desk was clean so they didn't get a security violation.

As a contractor, life is a little different. Since you are a non-permanent part of the workforce, you can sometimes feel (and are sometimes treated) like a second-class citizen. You don't get invited to some meetings or celebrations. The management of the company isn't supposed to talk to you, but instead is supposed to talk to your contracting company's management, who would talk to you. Most of the people there, however, didn't treat you any differently and were very nice to work with.

Working for a more formal company has a different feel. There was a dress code, so my jeans and t-shirts (dozens of them) were relegated to weekends. I had to go out and buy some more clothes to wear just for work. Although individual work hours were flexible, the requirement of working forty hours per week – no more, no less – drove me crazy. You were required to fill out a time sheet for both companies listing the charge numbers of the projects you were working on.

Now, I've always been a diligent worker and put in more than my required forty hours a week, but I've never really been made very conscious of it. In past jobs, when I had a ten or twenty minute commute, I'd go into work around 8 or 9, have lunch out, and work until 6pm. I'd think about work things on the way home and felt secure in the knowledge that my company was getting their money's worth from me. At Rocky, however, since their money comes from the government or another buyer, they track things down to the tenth of an hour. You don't work overtime without approval, but need to get your time in. My commute also went from 10 minutes each way to 45. Between the increased commuting time and my other life responsibilities, I would eat lunch at my desk every day doing work so I didn't have to work any later. The rest of my life also became about preparing to go to work. I would iron my clothes, make my lunch, and pretty much think about work all the time. However, this was thinking about working and not thinking about the work itself. I'm happy to solve problems away from work. I can decide whether I want to spend the time thinking about a problem solution or what I want to get done next week. This was time worrying and thinking about getting to work and getting my time in and that made me miserable. Everyone at work was always talking about time, too – when they were going to leave, how much overtime they might need to put in, if permitted, etc. I've never been anywhere that was so time-related and I felt like salaried people shouldn't feel that way. I thought it cut into their productivity and made the place feel like an "us" (the workers) and "them" (the management) kind of place.

Before you go to work for a place like this, you should think about whether this environment is right for you. For me, it definitely wasn't. I found it stressful and it invaded the rest of my life more than work should.

Defense and government contractors are also subject to much more rigid processes. This was the kind of place that CMMI belonged (see the chapter on software processes), partly because your ability to talk to the "customer" was always more difficult. You also had to figure out who your customer was at any particular time. For the project I was on, the military gave requirements to Rocky International who was the main provider of the product (e.g. a truck). Rocky had a team (the general contractor team) that would then give requirements to another part of Rocky for that part (e.g. the dashboard) of the whole product. Then the dashboard team had a software development team, software verification (SV) team, systems engineering (Systems) team, and quality assurance (QA) team. Working on the software development team, our customer was sometimes the SV team, sometimes the Systems team, and sometimes the general contractor team. Ultimately, of course, the military was the customer, but whenever someone used the word "customer," I would have to ask who it was at the moment. Confused? So was I.

On the plus side, some of the work there was very cool. Despite the enormous amount of process involved with writing flight quality code, it was a lot of fun testing out code on a flight simulator. My occasional forays into the lab to do this made some of the increased rigor bearable.

As a sub-contractor, although I was treated well by my colleagues at Rocky, I had less of a feeling of satisfaction as I was not really part of the company. This is something else to consider if you're offered a consulting or contracting job. If you like going to work, doing what you're told, working towards 40 hours a week, and leaving your work at the office (other than how to get your forty hours in), this might be great for you. If you like having more of an emotional investment in what you're doing, you may want to reconsider.

Discussion and Thought Questions

1. Are job security, benefits, and a good salary more or less important to you than a fast-moving environment and the potential to feel like you really contribute to the bottom line?

2. Will you be upset if you have to look for another job in two years or think of it as another opportunity to find something else interesting to work on?

3. What type of career ladder are you looking for? Larger companies may have a more formal path you can follow, including training. Smaller companies may let you expand your responsibilities more easily, but have less guidance.

What are They Paying You for Anyway?

This section of the book has a mix of topics. I start with a description of the three greatest foul-ups I've seen in my years on the job. Next, I talk about benefits. I end up talking about ethics. It's a loose thread that ties these topics together, I admit.

Chapter 5: For Richer, For Poorer - How to lose millions of dollars

Failing to learn from failure is the biggest crime of all.

- The author

Okay, I didn't personally lose millions of dollars, but I got to watch it happen three different ways. If you're the CEO of a company or hope to become one, here are some mistakes not to make. I'll tell the stories in the order that they happened. Some of the information contained here is second hand and may therefore be somewhat inaccurate. Although some details may be wrong, these things did happen and the lessons to be learned are the same regardless.

We Create Our Own Competition

Dylan International was looking for a way to speed the design of their large heat exchangers. The design of these is fairly straightforward, but requires numerous calculations and decisions, and takes time. Generating a quote for a customer would take about a week to do a basic design. They felt, however, that since most of the computations and design variations were well understood, that the process could be automated. They were working with CompuCAD, a large CAD company, in the mid-1980s and arranged via a contract to have them deliver a system that would perform the task. Unfortunately, the CompuCAD salesman had oversold their capabilities a bit and they couldn't do what was required. They approached a couple of local researchers, one of them Barry Rose, and gave them the seed money to work up a solution. ICON Corporation was born. They produced a system that would indeed solve the problem, but it ended up costing CompuCAD a great deal of money (more than they were to earn on the contract) to satisfy Dylan.

The system was capable of performing the design based on input from a salesman that was filled in on a standard form.

But now, instead of taking a week to create a proposal for the customer, the system could actually perform an entire detailed design in a few minutes. This made their proposals both more accurate and much faster so they could increase the number of proposals that they could work on.

The group Vice President within Dylan, Bucky Keys, wanted to buy more systems from ICON to use in other parts of the company. Barry Rose made him an offer he couldn't believe – 50 systems for $15 million. Bucky essentially told him to stuff it and said he could build the system himself for less and Whistler Technology was born. Not only did ICON end up losing the sale of additional copies of their system to Dylan International, but they had now created their own competition, costing them even more money.

Would You Like to Buy This? Nobody Else Seems to Want it

When I went to work for Ram Technology, they had recently been acquired by the Maclean Corporation. It seemed like a very good fit. Ram was involved with the creation of finite element meshes and the display of the analysis results, while Maclean performed the actual analysis. Unfortunately, like many acquisitions, if you don't take the time to do a good job on the integration of the companies, especially in sales and marketing, then you can start to flounder. After about a year, the Ram software wasn't selling very well and then Maclean merged with another company that had different, but related software to Ram. They got most of the attention and Ram's sales got even worse. Finally, Maclean announced that they were likely to discontinue development of Ram's software after the next release.

A couple of months later, I was sitting in the audience of the company's annual technical meeting and heard the President of the Maclean Corporation say, "Sales of the Ram software have not been doing as well as we hoped lately. We are, therefore, going to discontinue further development."

Talk about a self-fulfilling prophecy. If I told you that I wasn't going to do any more development of a software product and was planning to discontinue it shortly, would you buy it? Of course not.

Mergers and acquisitions are a mixed bag. Some are well designed and executed; some are well-intentioned, but poorly executed. If you want to merge with or take over another company, you should carefully sweat the details from software development to marketing and sales. Otherwise, you're wasting your time and money.

Taking on Goliath

My final, most recent, and most incredible tale involves the BDI company. I left Ram and Maclean after the President's speech I just told you about and went down the street to BDI. BDI had started as a consulting and contracting company that wrote software for use in other people's software. Eventually, the leaders of the company decided that it was time to try it on their own. They developed a fantastic system called Trident that was very easy to use and absolutely blew me away the first time I saw it.

I joined them shortly after the first release of their system. Sales were going okay, but they had their sights on bigger and better things and the next release was going to be very ambitious. Shortly after I joined, the President of BDI, Hal Samson, called everyone together for a company meeting. He told us that he had been to visit the CEO of Ottobon Software, who had offered him $150 million (other people remember this number as $50 million among other numbers, but the precise figure isn't important) for BDI. It was an astronomical number for a company of only 40 people with sales just starting to move. The thing that really blew me away was that he turned it down! He told us that this offer was a validation that what we were doing was on target and had great potential. What could be more inspiring? I couldn't wait to get my stock options in a few months and see what we could make of the company. I also figured that maybe I had finally become part of a company that was really going to hit it big.

The next couple of months were great fun as we got started. We worked on some terrific stuff and were excited about the coming release. Unfortunately, after doing some estimation on the work involved, the managers concluded that it would take 11 months of development work. Hal said we needed it in half that time. We buckled down as best as we could and got to work. Not too long into the development cycle, changes started happening. Now, instead of one product with two variations, Trident Standard and Professional, we needed to produce three products with two variations each.

One of these new products was a very inexpensive version of our software for generating web page content. Unfortunately it was so cheap that Hal said we would lose money on every copy. I was confused by this decision, but figured he must know what he was doing or he wouldn't be doing it. We developers did joke about it, however. How would we make money on this new product? The answer was simple: volume.

We hired more developers for the office in Georgia (we were in New York) and they started on some of the new functionality. Hal said this next version needed to hit the ball out of the park and therefore needed even more functionality than we had initially planned. This put us even further behind schedule, but we plunged ahead anyway. Several months after our alleged deadline, as we finally had most of our functionality complete and were trying to stabilize the system and fix the bugs, Hal threw another curve ball. In order to make the sales numbers, we needed to run not only on Windows95, which we were designed for, but also Windows 3.1. This was a monumental change that would ripple throughout the entire system. We started to integrate a package from Microsoft that would help, but our system and the Microsoft software was extremely buggy. The system had taken a giant leap backwards and wouldn't be ready for release for another three months or so.

Meanwhile, I had received my stock options – a whopping 160 shares! Now if it had been like Google stock, it might have had promise, but this was BDI. I was underwhelmed.

As time passed, BDI was defaulting on contracts that they had signed with software distributors. They had hoped to be included on some hardware as trial software, but now there wasn't any software to ship. Hal pushed us to work harder. Nights and weekends were already the standard and had been for a while so I didn't know what more we could do. To spur us on to even more heroic effort he told us that our stock would be worth $1000 per share when we hit it big. Considering that there were one million shares, including my whopping 160, that meant the company would someday be worth one billion dollars. Somehow, I didn't see it happening, but we plugged along anyway.

With the passage of more time and the bleeding of money, things were getting desperate. We were still trying to stabilize the software and get it ready for release. As we finally got to the point where we could think about shipping, Hal informed us that another offer had been made for the company. We were going to be sold. This offer, however, wasn't going to be worth anything near what Ottobon had offered, although the number was never revealed.

Although the deal was signed with the intent to close the acquisition within sixty days, the company buying BDI wanted three things. One, re-brand the application with their company logo and name. Two and three, improve performance and fix more bugs. Naturally, when you try to do any of these things, the software goes into flux again. We proceeded to do what was requested of us, despite our protestations that it didn't sound like a very good idea. Naturally, the deal fell through after a few weeks. It took a few more weeks to get the system stable and finally ready to release, many months late. BDI had people selling the software over the phone in order to bring in money. The employees were all required to take a temporary twenty five percent pay cut to save the company money.

While all of this was going on, my manager, Harry Feldman, had been talking to an old friend, who now worked for Ottobon. He had convinced Ottobon that they could get the brains behind the BDI software by simply offering to hire us all.

Hal, however, was also still working on salvaging what he could of his company. Just as Harry had been working with Ottobon, Hal had been talking to Visceral Systems to have them buy BDI. Hal called another company meeting and told us that we had been sold again. However, things were more interesting this time and there were choices to make. We could stay with the company and join Visceral or we could go to work for Ottobon. Before we decided, we would be able to talk to people at both companies and decide which company was most appealing. This came with several words of caution, however. This is the gist of Hal's words as best as I can remember.

> "Folks, I would love to have you all stay with me and begin working with Visceral, but I understand that Ottobon also sounds very appealing. Let me warn you that Ottobon is a very big company and I will not be around to protect you. Let me also tell you a story about a meeting that I had a couple of years ago with the CEO of Ottobon, Connie Bartram.
>
> I had flown out to California and called her office. Her secretary gave me directions to a restaurant where we would meet to discuss the acquisition of BDI. Unfortunately, I got lost along the way as the directions were fairly complicated. When I stopped to ask for directions, I was told that I was in completely the wrong place. So, I followed my new directions and arrived at the restaurant about an hour late. Even worse, I was really at another location of the restaurant chain. I got new directions and finally arrived about two hours late for my meeting.

Connie was sitting at the bar, looking very angry. Her first words to me were, 'Where the f*** have you been?' Although she calmed down after my explanation and we had a good conversation, I decided that this was not who I wanted to sell BDI to."

After the meeting, the engineers got to talking. Some were upset that Hal felt that we needed protection and couldn't survive in the "wild" of a big, bad company. I personally felt that here was a guy who, unfortunately, had managed to get lost and get insulted, and because of that, decided to turn down millions of dollars for his company. He was now losing his shirt and possibly half of his employees due to his own bad management and judgment. Finally, after thinking about the past year of poor decision making and constant pressure, I felt the decision was a pretty easy one. So did almost all of my colleagues; we all went to work for Ottobon.

Visceral did continue to produce BDI's software, but it was eventually spun off into another company. Hal went on to start another consulting company whose major client was none other than Ottobon. Twelve years after his initial offer for BDI, he sold his new company to Ottobon.

Discussion and Thought Questions

1. Are you considering running your company into the ground? I didn't think so – good for you.

2. Are you overselling what you can deliver on a contract?

3. Are you publicly giving hints that your software product is undergoing major changes? Are you aware of how this may affect short-term sales?

4. If you're a manager, director, or CEO, are you making any of the mistakes that any of these CEOs did? Are you sure? Ask your employees to verify this.

Chapter 6: What's My Motivation? – Benefits

I told you I needed to feed my family. They offered me 3 years at $21 million. That's not going to cut it.

- NBA Star Latrell Sprewell

Just like an actor or basketball player, you need to decide what your motivation is. Is it the satisfaction of a job well done, the feeling of teamwork, padding your bank account, saving for retirement, paying for your children's educations, or something else? Are you, like Latrell Sprewell, worried about feeding your family on only seven million dollars a year? Who could blame you? In actuality, it's probably a combination of them all. In this chapter, we'll talk about some of the things that are available and what you can expect. Apologies in advance for all of the food-related topic headlines.

Meat and Potatoes

The one thing that regularly comes to mind when you're taking a new job or working at your current one is your salary. It's like

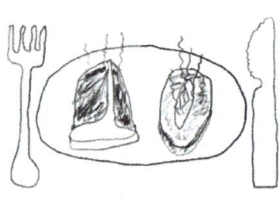

the basic meat and potatoes of your life. It's what you can count on week to week to pay the bills. In the software industry, salaries are pretty good, but that's not to say you can't get yourself into financial trouble. As any financial advisor will tell you, try to live within your means. Don't buy that new car until you've got some money in the bank to pay for it. Don't start ringing up major credit card debt.

When you think about your salary, you may want to compare it to the industry averages, which you can easily find out from some fine web sites. Keep in mind that salaries vary wildly between small and large companies, their sources of income, and their financial stability. Larger, more stable companies will usually pay a higher salary. Smaller companies will usually pay less, but sometimes give stock options as a performance incentive. More about this later. None of this is a hard and fast law – some companies pay much more or less than you might expect and this can vary with location, industry, and corporate culture.

When negotiating a salary, keep these words of advice in mind: in most salary negotiations, the first person to mention a dollar figure loses. Unfortunately, in many interview situations, your potential employer will ask what you made at your last job and/or what you're looking for. It's best to defer answering this question by stating that you're somewhat flexible (even if you're not) and that the total package you're offered is more important than just the salary. You might also say that it's too early to discuss this until you both find out if there's a good fit between you and the company.

Companies have wide, and I really mean *wide*, salary ranges for most positions. Consider that they have a number of people with varying experiences working there. They've gotten raises over the years and may be making a lot of money. At the same time, they may hire students out of college or graduate school and need to pay a competitive rate to attract new talent. It's not uncommon for a new hire out of college to make more than an employee who has only been there a couple of years. By the way, discussing salary with your colleagues is almost never a good idea – it almost always leads to someone getting upset about their current status.

When the company does make you an offer, realize that it's just that, an offer. It may or may not be an absolute, take it or leave it number, and it's usually not. At some companies, the salary ranges for a particular pay grade (a combination of experience, promotions, etc.) were around $40,000. For example, you might be talking about a possible salary from $80,000 to $120,000.

At one job interview, Bob was asked about his salary requirements. He deferred for a while, which was good. At one point, however, the head of the company asked him what he made at his last job. Bob could have deferred again, but felt that it was to his advantage to tell him. Why? Bob had been at his previous company for a few years and his salary had risen significantly. He knew that no other company in town would or could match it. On the other hand, he also wanted them to know that he was very good and wouldn't want to take too big of a pay cut. He also didn't want to move out of town. So, he felt the best negotiating tactic was to tell them what it was and force them to max out their offer. When Bob got an offer, it was more than he expected. It wasn't close to his previous salary, but it was reasonable and, higher than he expected. It was also higher than another company was offering him, so he took the job.

Their competitor, Endo, was also interested in Bob and when asked, he declined to mention salary to them. They made him an offer far below what he had been making. When he asked why, he was told that his experience wasn't that close of a match to what they needed (he hadn't written any embedded code), but after 6 months there would be a performance review and it might change then. He told them that the offer was far too low and the hiring manager immediately made an offer that was $2500 higher and offered him an extra week of vacation. Bob said he'd think about it. When the offer arrived in the mail, it was $5000 higher than their initial offer. He was about to take the job when the other offer came through.

The other thing related to salary that you can negotiate is the pay grade at which you start. A higher pay grade won't necessarily change your salary, but within companies, this can mean a bonus as a higher percentage of your salary, or more stock options that may be given on a yearly or more frequent basis. Additionally, companies strive to get their people moving towards the middle of their pay grade. If you start out as a junior, associate, or level one software engineer, the pay range for that grade might be $50,000 to $70,000. An offer of $60,000 already puts you in the middle. However, if you can convince them that your experience and potential warrants the pay grade of a staff engineer or level two software engineer, the range for that might be $60,000 to $80,000, putting you at the bottom. Next year your company reorganizes and you have a new manager. At raise time, he looks at your salary and says, "Hmm, you do great work and you're at the bottom of your pay grade, you deserve a good bump in salary. Oh, and since you're at grade two instead of grade one, I can give you a better bonus, too." Sweet.

Negotiating is expected nowadays and, as long as you are nice about it, won't influence your relationship with your future company. Remember, they already want you. All you're doing is trying to start out as high in the salary range as you can. If you manage to negotiate another five or ten thousand dollars up front, you've gotten the equivalent of two or three years of raises already built into your salary. That's your meat and potatoes, and as an old colleague used to point out, you can buy a lot of pizzas with that kind of money.

Duck Breast Cutlets Sautéed with Leeks and Wild Mushrooms Topped with a Raspberry Coulis

Since employee salaries are expected by the employees every year, your company needs to be sure that they can pay them every year. This is one reason why some companies don't want to give huge raises every year. So, how do you encourage and reward your employees when there's excellent corporate or personal performance? One answer is bonuses.

There are various types of bonuses that companies use. For employees who do an exemplary job on a particular project, there's the spot bonus. It's an "attaboy" to say thanks and to recognize that they really went beyond standard expectations.

For corporate performance, I've seen bonuses done two ways. The first way was a pay grade and salary based plan. This plan was funded when the company met or exceeded their financial goals for the year. As the company and your division met the sales expectations, the pot for your division began filling. The company made this publicly visible in an effort to encourage people to do what they could to help. At the end of the year, the pot was filtered down to the employees. Your bonus was then given somewhere in a range that was based on your pay grade. Lower pay grades, the junior engineers, could receive a bonus of around 10% of their salary. For higher grades, the senior engineers, it could go up to 20%. When the company had an extraordinary year, the bonuses were even higher than that.

The other bonus plan that many people really liked was the corporate-wide bonus. When the company met its goal for the year, everyone from the CEO down to the janitors got the same bonus. While it wasn't a huge amount of money, the fact that everyone shared the same amount was kind of cool.

Fettuccini Alfredo

A few years ago, The Center for Science in the Public Interest called *fettuccini alfredo* a "heart attack on a plate." This brings up the topic of health insurance. Although you may or may not be worried about this now, eventually you will be. Most companies have a health care plan. Some provide health insurance that doesn't cost you anything while some require you to pay a portion of it from your paycheck. On the plus side, it's taken out of your pay before you pay taxes on the money, so that saves you some money, but the minus side is that it's usually on the order of $100 to $200 per month or more. Some companies will pay for all of the cost of the employee alone and charge you only for the rest of your family. Domestic partners, such as your life partner that you're not married to or aren't permitted by law to marry, are often able to be covered by your policy. If your spouse or life partner has insurance that's better or cheaper than yours, your company will allow you to "opt out" of your coverage and some companies will actually pay you to do so. This should definitely be considered when you are weighing your options.

In addition to health insurance, many places offer dental insurance. In my experience, this is usually the worst insurance imaginable. I don't know how they get away with the high fees and low benefits that they provide. For example, my wife's dental insurance is free for her, but costs money to cover the family. For having a cavity filled, my wife was charged $120 and insurance covered $20. Would you pay anything extra out of your paycheck for this? We're not. I don't know why more places don't simply cover their employee's dental insurance with a pool of their own money. The company would save money on insurance and employees would get more money out of it.

Most companies offer long-term disability insurance and life insurance and you should almost always accept whatever the company is going to pay for without anything out of your pocket.

Some companies are starting to offer more insurance options that are a bit unusual. Your company may offer pet care insurance, legal insurance, homeowners, or car insurance. These are usually not subsidized like health insurance, so they tend to be more expensive.

A Hamburger on Tuesday

I'm mixing up an old *Popeye* quote from a character named Wimpy – my apologies to the purists out there. I don't know anyone who doesn't love stock options, especially when the company gives them out on a regular basis. Stock options are the *option* to buy a stock at a later date for a pre-determined price. For example, your company may give you 100 options at $10/share. It may be a while before you are allowed to "exercise" the options, though, and this is called the *vesting period*. Most stock options have a vesting period of a year or more, so you can only imagine the money you'll make on them until they are vested. Now, let's say three years down the road, you're fully vested and can now exercise all of your options. The stock price is now $20/share. You get to use your options to buy them at $10. That's a tidy profit of $1000 and you didn't have any risk at all. Well, there's a risk that the stock price would be lower than your option price in which case you simply wouldn't exercise them.

Stock options are a great incentive. They keep you looking at what the company is doing and hoping for a day in the future when you can sell them or keep waiting for them to go up.

When you are offered a job at a company, you may be given a batch of options and you may be able to negotiate a few more. They may also be given out periodically during your tenure.

The Vending Machine

If your company is publicly traded, you may be given the opportunity to buy stock (not options, but actual shares of stock) as part of your retirement plan or as part of your regular pay. Some plans are better than others and you should be certain not to place all of your eggs in one basket, lest you find out you've joined the son of Enron.

At Whistler, Bob was allowed to put 25% of his retirement savings into company stock. It worked out very well, too.

At another company there was a stock purchase plan which was far more generous, however. Instead of being part of your retirement plan, this operated more like a high interest savings plan. Here's how it worked. The plan operated in six month periods. You could invest up to 15% of your pre-tax salary (but it was taken out after taxes) into the plan. Your purchase price for the stock was the lower of the prices at the beginning and end of the six month period, minus 15%. So, even if the stock price went down over the six months, you would still make 15% on your money. If that wasn't good enough, you locked in your lowest purchase price for two years. There were times when people were able to triple their investment.

The funniest part is that when Bob first started working there, his wife thought that it was too good to be true. "There must be some sort of catch," she said.

"Don't you think that if it were some kind of racket that the other employees of the company would have spread the news by now? Besides, why would your own company want to rip off its employees," he replied.

64

I know what you're thinking. Didn't Enron (although it was for their 401K plan) essentially do that? Yup. So you need to decide if you're going to invest all of your money in one place or just some of it.

Soft Foods Only, Please. I Left My Dentures at Home

As you get older, your retirement planning enters the forefront of your thinking. When you're younger, however, this seems like a distant future that you can worry about when you're "older". Social Security is becoming less secure by the year. My Social Security statement from 2004 said that the Social Security System would be out of money by 2042, in 2006 it said it would be out of money in 2040, and in 2007 it was back up to 2041. Doesn't sound very promising, does it? Therefore, I strongly recommend at any age that you start investing the most money possible in your company's retirement plan. For the most part, this consists of a 401K plan.

Money from your paycheck is taken out before taxes and put into a set of investments for you. You get to decide the allocation of the money as aggressively or conservatively as you wish. Nowadays, many of these plans are managed by a major mutual fund company such as Vanguard or Fidelity. This gives you a variety of funds to choose from. When you're young, being more aggressive can really set you up well for later in life. Additionally, if you put money in when you're young, your money will be working harder for you and you may be able to back off a bit later, when you have a family and need the money to pay the bills. Most companies will match a certain amount of your personal investment. Not investing enough to use the entire company match is just leaving money on the table.

Look at the options for investment that you have. If you don't like them, then you should contact your plan administrator and tell them what you're looking for. When I started at BDI the stock market was booming. I was able to get some incredible returns on my personal investments, like twenty or thirty percent on some of them. However, the best options on the company's 401K plan were only returning ten percent. I went to talk to our HR person. She explained that most of the people at the company were conservative investors. OK, I thought, but you're not even offering an option for the more aggressively minded people and I said so. She looked into it and had a few options added for us.

When you get your quarterly statement, be sure to take a careful look at how things are performing and that your portfolio makes sense. At BDI, they had hired a 401K accounting firm to track everyone's investments. I had chosen some more aggressive things at this point, but my portfolio's balance didn't seem quite right to me. It seemed like my money just didn't grow as much as it should have. It turned out that the brilliant accounting firm that they had hired had just treated everyone's money as one big pool. They then divided all of the earnings of all the investments proportional to the amount we had in the plan. This meant that a conservative investor who should have gotten five percent on his investments was getting ten percent and although I should have gotten twenty percent, I was also getting ten percent! We had our HR person straighten out the accountants and a couple of months later the problem was corrected.

Just Desserts

Some of my favorite memories of work are not being there. When you've been working hard for months on end, nothing is better than saying goodbye to everyone and everything and taking a nice vacation. Good companies know that you'll be more productive at work if you get away, have some fun, and forget about work for a while. Don't be afraid to use your vacation time (unless your boss is looking for an excuse to screw you) and enjoy life for a while. Most places give you between two and three weeks per year when you start. After a few years, you may get another week or a few days and eventually max out at four or five weeks. When you start a new job, see if you can negotiate an extra week of vacation. If your potential manager looks at you with the thought that you're a slacker you can tell him that, of course, this is mainly for use after you've been there a while and are being very productive in your new position.

At one company, everyone received 12 days a year and it never went up. On the plus side, every four years, you could take a sabbatical for six weeks. Unlike an academic sabbatical, you weren't expected to do any work or research. This was just six weeks of continuous vacation. I went to Alaska on one of mine; Japan on the other. Some of my colleagues went to Europe, India, Thailand, China, or just stayed home and simply enjoyed not working.

If you find a company that offers this, consider yourself lucky.

Alka Seltzer

Especially if you have stock options or a stock purchase plan, it's vital to do your taxes very carefully or have someone else do them for you. One year, I didn't realize that part of my stock purchase plan profits had already been added to my income for the year. I would never have guessed this and proceeded to pay a lot of taxes because I was being taxed twice on the same money, once on the income it added, and once on the capital gains I accounted for. It wasn't until I was doing my taxes the next year that my tax software asked me a question that made me look very carefully at my W2 form. It was then that I noticed this unexpected item. I filed an amended return for the previous year and promptly told all of my colleagues who were very grateful and filed

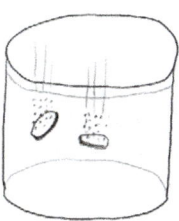

amended returns as well. The government, who always finds out that I've made a mistake in my own favor, didn't catch it either. Big surprise.

If you get and exercise stock options, note that there are different kinds and that they have different tax implications as well. Some are taxed as soon as they are exercised, so you'll want to avoid paying double taxes on that income. If you've already messed up your taxes in a previous year, file an amended return and you can buy me a beer if I've alerted you to the problem. You're welcome.

Discussion and Thought Questions

1. What benefits do you think are the most valuable for you personally? Will these play a role in your consideration of your next job?

2. Are you worried that taking a vacation or sabbatical will cost you your job when you return? Talk to your manager and some colleagues about this.

Chapter 7: Come On, Just This Once? – Ethics

No one's ever gonna know.

- Famous last words of many ex-employees.

With the ever-increasing litigiousness of our society, companies are often forced to take steps to protect themselves. They make their managers take classes, attend seminars, or read material on legal practices, racial bias and tolerance, and how to ask interview questions that don't violate laws. Did you know that you shouldn't ask someone about their spouse or children in an interview? If it turns out that they're gay and you don't hire them, they could sue you for discriminatory hiring practices.

But That's Personal

Almost everyone I know receives and sends out personal email at work. At one company, I didn't have a choice. I wasn't permitted to access my personal email account from the company's network, so I occasionally had to send out stuff using my work account. The two things you need to know about this are:

1. Nothing's personal at work in an email. The company is free to scan your incoming and outgoing email to make sure you're not divulging company secrets or writing a soft porn message to your girlfriend about what you'd like to do to her when you get home.

2. It's usually against company policy to use work email for personal business. The same goes for use of the internet.

All of your web site access may be monitored as well. If you decide to go trolling for porn at work, expect to get caught and either reprimanded or fired. One company I worked for would pop up a web page that said the content you were trying to access was considered inappropriate and wouldn't let you view the page. This would also happen whenever I tried to look at the homepage for my Judo club, which I assure you doesn't have any inappropriate content. However, the company's web blocker didn't allow me access. What could I say? I couldn't ask them to unblock it either. I really had no right to be spending time at work checking some piece of information that wasn't related to work anyway.

I Know a Secret

Your company will often tell you things that shouldn't be repeated outside of work. You may find out about an upcoming corporate acquisition, for example. If you tell someone else about this, they may use this to make money on that company's stock. If you try to do the same thing, you can be prosecuted for insider trading. The answer is simple, don't deal with any stocks of companies that your company does business with unless you can say with absolute certainty that you don't have any information about what's going on that isn't publicly available. Chances are that you won't be dealing in volumes of stock that will attract any attention, but make sure you're clean in this respect, nonetheless.

Occasionally, an officer of the company, e.g. the CEO, may send out a message. It may detail the corporate strategy for the coming months or years and speculate on the health of the company. Anything you get from the company is private to the company and anything that they want to broadcast to the world will be handled so you don't have to worry about it. At one company, a message came out that fit this description perfectly. Later that day, the message appeared verbatim on a Yahoo! message board. The CEO sent out a scathing message to the entire company about keeping these kinds of things confidential. I suspected that the culprit was only trying to be a big shot, "I know something you don't know" kind of person. Although the person's identity on the message board was a nondescript nickname and they had no personal information, the company found the person the next day and they were summarily fired on the spot.

No One's Going to Miss This

It goes without saying that you shouldn't steal things from your company. This goes for office supplies as well as major equipment. You should know that making personal copies on the company copier is considered theft by most experts in this area. Basic office supplies such as pens also belong to the company.

There are extremes to this and sometimes it becomes impractical to not use something that the company has. My advice, don't abuse your privileges and give your administrative assistant a dollar to put in the petty cash fund now and then to cover your stuff. You'll have a clear conscience.

What Happens Here Stays Here

Technically, anything that you produce on a company computer also belongs to the company. Many companies have a written policy on this, too. If you decide that you're going to use your company laptop to work at home on your next prototype for a brilliant product, they may end up owning it. Check your policy agreements or call the HR department. Unless it's a project for charity, you may have a problem and knowing this up front may save you a lot of headaches later.

Also, anything that you learn at your company may be proprietary information that you can't use elsewhere. I'm not saying that your experience in Java coding stays behind when you leave, but if your company uses a proprietary algorithm in some of their work, that belongs to the company. Even though you may remember it when you leave, you're probably not allowed to use it. Consult with an attorney if you're not sure about something.

But It Said It Was Free

One of the diciest things you can deal with nowadays is freeware. There's a lot of great stuff on the Internet that's free for you to download and use. You may be tempted to use this at work, whether it's a Python implementation for a script that only you will ever see or a utility you'd like to include with a shipping application. Everything you download has a license file or a EULA (end user license agreement.) No matter what you think you know about these things, you should run it past the legal department first (assuming your company has one). This covers your butt and the company's as well. You'd be surprised what they won't let you use, even though you can't imagine why they won't let you use it.

Her Ass

There's a big difference between a complement and harassment. Some people know this difference and some don't. As a man and a former manager, I've had the pleasure of working with many women over the years. I've also tried to be conscious of the things that I've said and done around women and sometimes I've approached the line with a comment or a joke that really wasn't meant to insult anyone. Fortunately, these people knew me well and knew that my intent was never to harass or insult anyone.

For example, it's reasonable to pay someone a compliment in the same way that you might compliment a personal friend. If a colleague comes in wearing a new dress and looks nice in it, it's okay to say, "Mary, that's a very nice dress. Is it new?" It's hard to imagine someone taking offense at that comment and you've noticed that someone you work with is wearing something nice. However, saying, "Hey Mary. You look totally hot in that dress," is getting closer to the line of what's reasonable. If you're thinking about saying anything that starts with, "Hey Mary, I'd like to... ," then you're about to cross it.

What is considered harassment nowadays has greatly expanded. Generally, anything that makes the workplace less than hospitable to work in is now considered harassment. Jokes or comments on someone's race, sexual orientation, religion, or gender are just on the edge of where harassment begins. If you make sexual comments or requests to a colleague that makes them uncomfortable, you are crossing the line. If you are on the receiving end of something like this, you must start by telling the offender that their behavior makes you uncomfortable and that they should stop. If the behavior continues, then you should consult with a representative from Human Resources. By the same token, if someone else tells you that you are making them uncomfortable, you should stop.

Dewey Defeats Truman!

I can't remember who first told me this, but these are words to live by: "Don't do anything that you wouldn't want to have show up in a headline on the front page of the newspaper." Nowadays, I guess that would change to "the home page of CNN.com," but the idea is the same. If you're worried about something you're doing from an ethical standpoint, consult your manager or the legal department of your company.

Discussion and Thought Questions

1. Are you careful about what you tell friends and family that your company is doing? Do you tell anyone specific dates or details of major announcements that you may be privy to?

2. Are you careful to consider what a person of the opposite gender may think about a forwarded email or a comment you are making?

3. Are you sensitive to the feelings of a particularly religious person in your office?

Can't I Just Wear Cologne?

A friend of mine asked his wife, "Honey, do you think I should wear cologne?" She replied, "No, I think you should work with other people." I thought that was hilarious, but I know these people. You don't so you're probably just groaning. Tomorrow you'll tell this joke to all the folks at work anyway, you hypocrite.

After reading this section, you may just wish you could work alone. There are some great stories of some classic folks I've worked with over the years. Along the way, I hope you get a feel for the different people and their responsibilities (whether they choose to accept them or not.)

Chapter 8: Your Definition Goes Here – Marketing

The software should just know *that.*

- A few marketing people I've known.

No great marketing decisions have ever been made on quantitative data.

- John Scully

It took me a long time to learn the difference between in-bound marketing and out-bound and the people who did the jobs. In-bound marketing is taking the needs of the customer and determining the software solutions that will meet those needs. Out-bound marketing is taking the software that you've developed and helping the salesmen sell it.

My Qualifications Are – Um...

Like many jobs in this world, there are no qualifications to become a marketing person. Kind of like show business, you just need a big break. Of course, once you've gotten your first gig as a marketing person, your qualifications are now built upon that first job. I'm not saying that there's anything terribly wrong with any of this. I was trained as a mechanical engineer and moved into software, so I can't throw very big stones at the marketing folks. On the other hand, once you've decided to pursue a particular field, it makes sense to become very good at it. Study it. The most respected marketing folks are those who don't always have an answer for everything, say "I don't know" when they really don't, and admit when they were clueless about something.

The Importance of Being Earnest

Since there are different kinds of marketing and different backgrounds to the marketing people, it's an interesting and varied field. Additionally, software marketing is different in some respects from other fields because software is so malleable and often has so many features. Ask a person who specializes in marketing toothpaste if their brand will whiten your teeth and you'll probably get a "yes." Ask them how and they'll either say, "It removes surface stains" or "It gently and safely bleaches them." Now, ask a person who markets software if their application will make you more productive with the kind of work you do. You'll probably get a "yes." After that, it gets a lot more complicated. Chances are that their software *will* have some productivity enhancement for you. Chances are also that if you start asking more specific questions like, "We need to import BFD files, run a PTR analysis on it using some custom parameters, and output BMOC files. Can you do that?" Well, first of all, the marketing person may not know. Secondly, they may know that you can import and export files, but not necessarily those formats. They figure that the software guys can add that in the next release if there's a big sale at stake anyway. After all, you don't want to lose a customer, do you?

That's not to say that marketing folks are dishonest, conniving, or anything else. However, it is their job to help sell you the software. It is, therefore, the customer's job to make sure that the software lives up to the claims that are made. Nowadays, it's almost always possible to try software before you buy it so you can prove that it will solve your problem.

Marketing is important to software companies. If you're selling software, you want to present a certain image of your company and your product. If you're selling software games, then you want your potential buyers to know that your graphics are amazing, the play is fun, it's easy to get started with, but it's deep and you won't get bored. If you're selling a word processor, you want your customers to know that it can import and export anything that's thrown at it, you can format their documents in amazing ways, and that you'll help them create whatever they can dream up with ease and speed.

Since there are many aspects to marketing, the needs of your company will change at various points during its life and during each product's life cycle. Additionally, not every company needs the same kind of marketing work. If you run a small software consulting company, your marketing needs will be based on selling your services as knowledgeable, competent, responsible, and timely developers. If you sell off-the-shelf software, you'll need to have input from customers on the next release, feedback from customers on the current release, advertising for the current release, brochures and demos for the salespeople to use, and information available on your website for potential buyers to download.

Especially if your company or group is small, you need the right kind of marketing for your particular situation and people with a clue to carry it off. There's no reason to have your only marketing person creating a beautiful brochure to sell your product if you're just getting your company off the ground and don't have a product yet. They should be determining the target market, talking to your eventual customers, and evaluating the competition.

At the Whims of Marketing

Most of the time, especially if your company isn't huge, your marketing people will play multiple roles. They will start by helping to determine what you should have in your next release of the software. Inevitably this will be at least twice, but possibly three to five times as much as you can produce in the time frame in which they'd like it done (no, I'm not making this up). After this, it looks pretty much like the World Championship of Poker, minus the cards and chips, but with similar sums of money lying in the balance.

Here's a typical conversation between marketing and software at the beginning of a new release.

Now the parties split up and start the details of their work. The marketing folks want every feature on the approved list to be polished, perfect, and gorgeous. The software developers want the same thing, but realize that with the time constraints, the simplest answer to most of the needed functionality will have to do. Ironically, that usually ends up being the most useful functionality.

Unfortunately, this is what happens in the next meeting of the minds.

Clearly this is a bit of an exaggeration, but not as much as you might think. Marketing always wants more features in less time. It's their job to try to have the most functionality to sell. Software development always wants more time and less features. It's their job to produce high quality software on time. They know that estimating the time to write software is almost impossible to get right. They also know that no matter how hard they might try, the estimates will be too low and there will be tons of bugs to fix in the end.

Sometimes marketing folks think that the software developers just sit around playing video games most of the time and overestimate the time required to do the work to leave more time for playing around. At the same time, the software folks can develop a sense of mistrust of the marketing folks as dreamers. Management should do their best to explain that everyone's goal is the same in the end - produce a working piece of software that meets the customer's requirements in an acceptable time period.

I've had countless conversations with people who don't actually write software. They are frequently unable to understand why building software isn't like building a house, bridge, or tunnel. A builder can give you an estimate on when your house will be done. They have a standard checklist of things that need to happen and it's a well-understood problem. Unfortunately, software simply isn't like houses. Sure, there are standard checklists for general tasks to be done, but while you might be able to boil all of your programming tasks down to a checklist, the time estimates are still just estimates and are often off by days and weeks, even for a single task. The state of the art in software just isn't to the point of perfect estimates. For that matter, weather, labor issues, and other factors can set houses, buildings, and other construction projects (ever heard of the Big Dig?) way over budget and time.

The answer is that as software developers, you must defend your estimates and time lines. You must insist on a reasonable level of quality in your software. You must insist on reasonable workloads and deadlines. Simply giving in to the marketing folks will cause pain. There are times when you're going to have to give in, but some marketing people will often tell you that it's a matter of corporate life and death to get this feature done by that date. If this happens too often, go find another place to work. Either your marketing people are really bad or your company is balanced too tenuously for any job security anyway. Whichever is the case, take back your sanity and find a reasonable place to work. The best marketing folks will work honestly and reasonably with software development and the customers.

The Izes of the March

I'm going to put on my business writer's hat for a minute now and introduce the "Izes" of the march. When planning a release, the folks who define the release should follow these three guidelines.

1. Minimize – Think about clean and simple features from a user's perspective. I've seen many times when the designers have come up with a feature that's overly complicated for end users because they didn't think that the developers could code up the simple answer. Also, try to minimize the "must-haves" in any release. You're more likely to have a quality release in a reasonable time period if there's flexibility built into the contents of the release. Perhaps this can be made easier by coming up with a theme for the release instead of just a bunch of disjoint features.

2. Prioritize – Unless there is a priority of importance to the features, the developers or their management will choose what to work on. Developers often work on the most interesting looking functionality or sometimes will just try to knock off the "low hanging fruit" or easiest features. The down side of this is that if you need to cut some features when time is running short, you may be stuck cutting the most important features. While it may be difficult, prioritize the features for the release and the arguments down the road will be far fewer.

3. Realize – Especially in the world of software development, nothing goes quite as planned. Some things will be done early, some late. If I were a betting man, I'd

always bet on late, because that's been my experience. As a designer, manager, or marketing person planning a release, realize that some things will likely have to be dropped or people are going to have to go on a death march. I'm in favor of being willing to cut functionality that's going to miss the code complete date.

This is My Document

At Ottobon, while working on my first product there, we rapidly grew our marketing department. The product was going to make a big splash (so we thought) and we were really trying our hardest to make it beat our competition. Unfortunately, our competition had around 300 people working on their product and we had about 50. Nonetheless, we had lots to do and some of it was marketing work. On this product, we worked with a few other small companies who were providing us with content that we would ship with our software. Naturally, we needed to have these companies conform to some standards or we'd have even more work on our hands. Did we really need to hire another marketing person to manage that one document? Apparently so.

One thing I've noticed is that there's no shortage of work to be done in any company. Be it software development, quality assurance, sales or marketing, there's always too much to do and too little time to do it. However, if you want to hire a whole bunch of marketing people all you have to do is hire the first one. The rest will appear like rabbits.

There's a Seeker Born Every Minute

Conferences and trade shows are great fun. Where else can you wander around, get free stuff from companies you have no interest in, and look at pretty women (or handsome guys) working the booths (we called them "booth-babes" – I know, politically incorrect) all day long? Now, if you're a vendor, you have a different goal in mind. You want to generate leads. A lead is anyone who hands you a business card or has you scan their trade show ID so you can send them literature or make a sales call. Most of those leads are crap. Also there's a big difference between a lead and a possible sale. We used to call a possible sale a "hot lead." They were mostly crap, too. You see, unfortunately, trade shows are also filled with people I call "Seekers."

Seekers are people who go to trade shows with a mission. Their mission is to find the software that will meet a very special set of requirements. They don't intend to buy it, just to find it. Therein lies the problem.

When I worked for Whistler, we made a very specialized product. It fit into a category known as knowledge-based engineering. This field still exists today with several companies still selling solutions quite similar to what we sold twenty years ago. It's very useful stuff, but because there's a lot of customization that the customer needs to do to apply it to their particular problem and you only need a small number of systems per company, they are very expensive.

Although I was a software developer, since we were a small startup division, almost everyone worked the booth at the trade shows that we went to. At first, it was kind of fun to talk to customers and tell them about our great software. We had nifty demos to show and made quite a production of it all. However, at trade show after trade show, I would describe to people what the software did and how it could help them. It was just too far ahead of its time for many people. (Note: we did not invent the technology, actually ICON did, but I'm sure they had similar issues at trade shows.)

Then, I met my first Seeker. One day at a trade show, a man approached me with a small shopping bag filled with free stuff from other booths and began to speak, "I'm looking for software that I can describe my engineering problems to. I'd like to be able to define parts and assemblies, give them attributes, create expressions for the relationship of the attributes, and automate some of my designs."

My jaw dropped and my heart raced as a man had just described our software. I excitedly told him what our software did and how it would solve his problem. I scanned his ID and made sure to mark him as a hot lead. Even as I did this, I knew that he wasn't really interested in buying it. He was just *looking* for it. Then he thanked me for my time and continued on his way. He and his company were never heard from again. I'm sure that after leaving the booth, happy to have found his Holy Grail, he was rapidly formulating the requirements for the next quest.

The people that you meet at tradeshows are a mixed bunch of people who are genuinely interested in what you have to sell and people looking for free t-shirts (I've got a drawer full of them). Much of the reason to be at a trade show in the first place is to simply create some marketing buzz. I'm not sure if it's worth the time and money spent, however. If you are at a trade show and are talking to customers, be helpful and informative, but don't get too excited if you run into a seeker. Keep this in mind and you'll rarely be disappointed.

What the Hell Are We Doing Here?

After doing my time working in our booth at various trade shows over a period of three years or so, I was beginning to tire of them. The leads generated didn't seem to help our sales much. Going to the trade shows was expensive and occasionally we'd end up at a show that we really didn't belong at. It's kind of like going to an auto parts store and seeing stuffed animals next to the motor oil. You might think that there's a reason that they're there, but you don't really care and just move on. Trade shows can be like that, too. Sometimes the trade show has changed its focus and sometimes you're just at the wrong one.

For example, our software ran on a machine called the Texas Instruments MicroExplorer. It was a supercharged Macintosh that ran LISP (the language our software was written in) on a special board. One year, we got a call from Apple. They wanted us to come to SIGGRAPH (a computer graphics tradeshow and conference) and be in their booth. I explained to the marketing person, Paul McCarthy, on the other end of the phone that we needed a TI MicroExplorer, not just a Mac. He said sure, that was fine, it would be there, and like a fool I believed him. When we showed up in Atlanta, I was shown to our station in the booth. It was clearly not the correct machine. I found someone from Apple and told them what the problem was and to whom I had spoken. Just as I was doing this, Paul McCarthy was walking by and said, "I'm Paul McCarthy and I've never heard about any of this!"

I replied, "I'm Bill Myers. We spoke a few weeks ago. Do you remember me asking you about a special machine that we needed?"

What could he say? He had to sheepishly back down. Unfortunately, I had to have my colleagues back in Cleveland send our machine down on the next plane. At least the monitor would work with our CPU, so that didn't need to be sent. The best part is that I got to spend a week in the Apple booth trying to show people some engineering software at a computer graphics show. The most commonly asked question that I got was, "What kind of monitor is that?"

Sometimes, as in this case, you'll end up going somewhere to build goodwill for your company and your product. Be careful to set your expectations accordingly. In this case, it would have simply been better to have thought about what we might really have gained from this particular show and politely declined.

Trust Me, You Belong at NCGA

Back in the late 1980's and early 1990's, there was another conference and trade show called the National Computer Graphics Association, or NCGA. We had gone there for a couple of years and had determined that the nature of it was changing so we wouldn't go back the next year.

During that year, we had hired Drew Bergman as our new marketing leader. He, in turn, hired a consultant, Hugh Gestit, to help him with a new approach to marketing our software. They came out with a very slick set of materials including videos, brochures, and a new buzzword for the type of software we produced. Buzzwords are often created by marketing people and they do serve a purpose. If you have a truly new kind of software, you may want to create a buzzword to describe it in a nutshell. The buzzword and materials that were chosen for our software, however, were a bit of a stretch, I'm afraid. It was probably enough to get people's attention, which may have been good enough, but I didn't feel like it really hit the target of what we really did and did best.

Anyway, we were at Autofact, a tradeshow in Detroit that we did fit in well with, and heard that we were going to NCGA again. As it turns out, our new consultant, Hugh, was on the board of the NCGA conference, so naturally he wanted us to go. I tracked down Drew to tell him that we had previously determined that NCGA didn't seem to be up our alley any more. Hugh happened to be drifting by and overheard me expressing my concerns. Hugh pointed at our new buzzword banner and our fancy booth displays and said, "Look at what you were showing last year and look at what you're showing now. Trust me, you belong at NCGA."

And there it was. What really mattered wasn't that the conference wasn't right for us in the past, but that we weren't right for the conference. With our new marketing buzzwords, we would take the place by storm. So we went. There weren't very many good customers to meet there, but we met with some people from the press. That became the positive takeaway from that conference.

We Need this Urgently, Let Me Know How I Can Hinder You

In many software companies, the businesspeople are the kings, although some are still run by the software folks who started them. As a software person, the sooner you come to terms with this, the better. You should still do your best to keep people honest, but the simple fact is that the marketing people often dictate what's going to happen.

The most difficult thing to deal with can be the "easy" projects. Since they're easy, they often come without the same level of design and specification as the more detailed projects. Furthermore, it's very easy to get yourself in the mindset that something will be easy to accomplish, so you don't really need a specification.

I once had a project that should have taken a couple of weeks to complete to create a trial version of our product. It was mandated by the marketing department and was supposed to be very important. I found a great product, Crocodile Security, which helped with the trial period and let the end users unlock the product with a registration key. I asked for some information from our marketing department including a small dialog design, verbiage for the dialog, and some titles to go on the product. The marketing folks were busy working on the new advertising campaign, so this never came.

The folks at Crocodile were going to provide the custom dialog for us and in the absence of a dialog design, created their own. I knew immediately that it wasn't going to pass muster with our marketing folks and forwarded it to them. Their response was that it didn't pass muster with them and should look a little like this and that – a textual description. I asked them once again for a drawing and the actual words and didn't get it. The next incarnation from Crocodile was better, but still not right (imagine!) Finally, our marketing folks came to the conclusion that if they didn't provide a picture and the text to go on it, that it would never be done correctly.

In the end, the project took almost two months. I kept my manager informed along the way so that I was covered. The moral here is simple: without a proper specification, you may end up going in circles for a while. If you want to get things done most efficiently when you're working with marketing, someone should write a specification and have it approved. You can make changes to it, but you'll likely get to the finish line sooner.

Let's Just Call it "Streamlined"

One small software group in a big company that made mostly large equipment had its challenges. One of those challenges was getting help with marketing. They wanted to produce a brochure for their product, so the marketing department for the group that made industrial-strength signal controllers got right on it. Bob gave them some preliminary photos to use and some information about the software and they got right to work. Bob told them that he wanted to improve the photos, but was told that once the photos were printed you wouldn't see any of the flaws that he wanted corrected. As he feared, the pictures looked like crap (in his opinion) and he thought they were rather obvious. In addition to this, there were extraneous pictures of heavy equipment that had absolutely nothing to do with the software.

The best part was in the text, however. On the last page of the brochure was this:

> Unlike other **less functional** software, the Product Name Here has all of the power you need to solve your prob-lems.

Of all the things to highlight, they picked the words "less functional" and saw nothing wrong with it.

It always pays to be a perfectionist when it comes to producing things that the customer will see. Bob should have insisted on giving higher quality pictures to the marketing folks in the first place. Secondly, they should have insisted on some more input to the design of the material.

FUD Power

I had been working for a while before hearing about and understanding FUD marketing. FUD stands for fear, uncertainty, and doubt. It's used by more powerful companies to squash competition. For example, let's say you're Minute Technology Company and you are coming out with a product that threatens the established leader, Goliath Corporation, in your field. You've got some novel functionality and are starting to look like you might be for real, rather than a flash in the pan. Your company could seriously cut into the profit margins of the Goliath. Well, Goliath simply puts out a press release stating that they will soon be releasing their new version of the product which will have all of that novel functionality and more. In actuality, Goliath may not have that functionality for a couple of years or even know how to go about incorporating it into their existing product. Of course, the customer doesn't know this. All they know is that if they just wait a little while, Goliath, a strong, established company will have their software out "soon" that will have the functionality they want. Goliath has just injected fear, uncertainty, and doubt into the mind of the customer who was considering buying software from Minute Tech.

If you work for Minute Technology, the first thing you should do is call out the FUD marketing as such. If you find that customers are being deterred from buying your product because of this, they should be politely reminded that you have the functionality in hand that can solve their problem and that Goliath Corporation is just sending up smoke and mirrors in a desperate attempt to keep their market share. When another company did this, we'd call it "selling vaporware." It's hard to fight FUD marketing from a big company. The best you can do is hope that potential customers will see it as it is and buy your product to show that this kind of thing won't work. Then, maybe, Goliath Corporation won't bother next time.

Miss America – Your Ideal

It's easy to poke fun at marketing folks, just read Dilbert for a while, for example. On the plus side, I have had the pleasure of working with some very good marketing people. They actually talk to customers and know what they want. They know how to get the attention of the customer and show them that we're selling them what they need. They create compelling advertising and literature. They admit what they know and what they don't. They work as hard to make the company successful as everyone else, don't point fingers when things go wrong, and share the blame as well as the kudos. If you find a person like this, who can do the little things while keeping the big picture in mind, keep her. She's worth a lot to your company. You've found a good one.

One marketing guy that I worked with came from a completely different background entirely. We were working on an architectural software product and Dave was an architect who came on board to help design and market the product. He brought in fellow architects to give lectures on various aspects of their work so that we software developers had an idea of the domain that our software was going to attack. He did the important stuff to get the software some visibility within the company and the marketplace.

Here He is – The Inventor of the Myers Artificial Heart

I hate advertising. My wife could tell you how I scream at the television after the beginning of the fiftieth showing of the same lawyer commercial – all in the same day. Advertising is a special function of marketing, so I'm including a short section about it here. I prefer my advertising to be either funny or informative, preferably both. Some of the crap that gets thrown my way, however, is infuriating or annoying, usually both.

With software, you have to be careful of the claims that are made and the ones that you make. Here's a rant of some things that advertisers do to cloud issues and give you a sense of something that's misleading.

Say it Again, Sam

I'm Dr. Know*. Did you know that it takes 64 ounces of water to make each line of code in your software? That's right, 64. The quality of that water also affects the quality of the code. That's why it's important to drink CodeWater®.

*Dr. Know received his Ph.D. in English from No. Such Online University. These statements have been carefully evaluated by our marketing department and have been found to be adequately misleading.

Did you know that 80% of all software developers don't test their code before checking it in? That's right, they check in their code and don't bother to try it out – compiling it is apparently good enough. Now you're thinking that it's fairly plausible. You've seen the system break enough times to know that there are colleagues that don't bother to test their changes (it goes without saying that *you'd* never do this). Now for the best part – I just made up that statistic. Yup, pulled it out of thin air. But, if I didn't tell you right here that it's crap, then you or someone else might have repeated it to someone else. Maybe later in this very book, I might have cited the same number again. After a while it becomes an accepted fact. I call this "Proof by Repeated Assertion." Something becomes perceived as true just because someone says it over and over again.

This happens all the time. In martial arts, it's a well-known "fact" that 90% of all fights end up on the ground. *Everyone* knows that they should drink 64 ounces of water in a day. I don't believe either statistic, but they're now part of the common knowledge base. When you see a statistic, verify its authenticity before you believe. Like the old saying, if it sounds too good to be true, it probably is. If you don't think that this could happen to you, then you're not thinking very hard.

They Call Me "Dr. Love"

Actually, I'm not really a doctor, I just play one at home. As a virtual doctor it never ceases to amaze me what some people try to get away with. I remember a television commercial for a weight-loss pill. This guy came on and said, "Hi, I'm Dr. Jim Beam and I'm here to tell you about an amazing new product. Blah, blah, blah." As soon as I saw it, I knew something was fishy. In fact, in the next commercial, he just said, "Hi, I'm Jim Beam…" I suspect that he had a Ph.D. in marketing and since a lot of people with Ph.D.s use the title "Dr.", it wasn't much of stretch for him. The problem is, he was perceived to be a medical doctor (a natural assumption) as he was advocating a weight-loss product. Now that just sounds dishonest, doesn't it?

I remember seeing an ad in a computer magazine. Members of the QA team were standing around a couple of computers. So far, you're thinking that sounds okay, aren't you? Here's the fun part. They were wearing lab coats. I don't know any software that can be infected by clothing, so this seemed a bit excessive to me. Maybe it was the Halloween issue of the magazine?

If someone has gone to school for a number of years to get their Ph.D., that's great. However, if it's not related to their purported area of expertise, then their opinion's probably no better than anyone else's. Furthermore, Ph.D. does not necessarily equal genius.

In This Corner, The Undisputed Heavyweight Champion

Some things are just impossible to dispute. Some things are just worded so well that you have to read between the lines. Who could dispute that I'm the inventor of the Myers Artificial Heart? (I envision a bucket with a sump pump in it). Who could argue that I was once a Heisman Trophy hopeful? Hell, I would have loved to have played football, which would have helped my chances, but a guy can hope, can't he?

How many times have you heard or read something in an advertisement that could be taken two ways? Rest assured, it's not by accident. Nowadays my favorite ads to hate are car commercials that advertise "available" features. They blend the word in so smoothly that it makes it seem as if you can go buy a really inexpensive car with all of this great stuff. Well, you can certainly buy the car, but it won't be inexpensive anymore. Those features aren't standard, they're "available."

Before you buy something, make sure that the claims can be backed up and that you know what is and isn't included as a standard feature. Before you sell something, make sure you can back up your information and what's standard, too. I stopped buying my tried and true tax software after the company started moving the functionality I needed to the most expensive version of the software. I went out one year and bought the same version that I had been using for ten years only to find that it didn't have the needed functionality anymore unless I coughed up another forty bucks. I did the computations myself and the next year bought their competitor's product. If you treat your customers well, they'll be fiercely loyal and forgive a few flaws, but screw them over even once and you could lose them forever.

Discussion and Thought Questions

1. What are your most pressing marketing needs right now? Are you in touch with your customers? Do you need to have more presence in the marketplace?

2. If you sell a product, do you know what the return on investment is?

3. Do you have good case studies for potential customers to look at that will help them understand why they, too, should buy your product?

Chapter 9: The Good, the Bad, and the Arguly – Sales

Life is a series of sales situations, and the answer is no if you don't ask.

- Patricia Fripp

I don't need to know how it works. I can sell anything.

- A few salesmen I've known.

In my career, I've worked for companies that have operated quite differently. My first company was a small division of much larger company. They knew nothing about producing or selling software. Since then, I've worked mostly for software companies. I'd swear that sometimes I thought that they also knew nothing about producing or selling software. Not all of the salesmen I have met are bad, uncaring, or clueless. Perhaps I've just met more than my share of them.

Let me also point out as a precursor that selling software isn't like selling some other products. One friend of mine used to sell food for a distributor. For him, I'm sure that selling some products as opposed to others really didn't matter much. Sure, he had to switch what market he was selling to and had to work with different kinds of customers. He'd develop a rapport with his customers, make sure they were satisfied with price and quality, and all was right with the world. I'm not saying it's easy; I know I couldn't do it. I'm just saying that knowing technical details of some products and what the customer might do with them doesn't apply to everything you might try to sell.

Software is different. For one thing, just about anyone can write software; all you need is a computer. You can probably get a free language compiler somewhere on the internet or you may even be able to use Visual Basic for Applications which comes embedded with Microsoft Word, Excel, and numerous other applications you might have on your computer already. Any customer you're trying to sell software to might just decide that they can write it themselves (I've done this a few times myself.) You have to show them that you're going to save them time and money.

Maybe what you've developed has technology that the customer hasn't thought of or doesn't have the expertise to develop. Your task in selling the software may be different depending on the type of software you have to offer. Most of the software that I've developed has been of a significant enough scale that customers weren't going to write it themselves. If you read the chapter on How to Lose Millions of Dollars, you'll see an incredible exception to this rule. Sometimes you're trying to sell to a customer that doesn't know that they need what you're selling. This can be a bit harder. Add to this that you may not only be selling them something they don't realize they need, but also that they're not just going to be able to install your software and it will start saving them money. What if it requires considerable customization? Sounds a little more daunting doesn't it?

The Good

I'll start this chapter with the best salespeople that I've worked with.

I'll Take it from Here

At Whistler, since the product was very programming oriented, most salesmen didn't understand the importance of what we were asking the customer to buy and what they had to do with it afterwards. We had one in particular, however, who did. Bob Steed would prepare for a sales call. He knew the software almost as well as our application engineers did. He attended our training classes so he'd know all of the latest features and how they worked. He would produce a focused demonstration of our software applied to the customer's problem. He'd call the developers and ask questions about how we might best attack a problem or see if we might be able to add some special code to the system to make solving a problem easier. He never promised a customer something we didn't have or couldn't have. He sold most of our software.

This and a Set of Ginsu Knives Might do the Trick

We hired a marketing guy named, Cade Madden, who had worked for another company in Cleveland. Cade had worked for Reliable Software Systems (RSS) and helped put together a very large proposal to solve a customer problem. RSS didn't have anywhere near the focused technology that we did. What we could have done for the same customer would probably have been better and ultimately cheaper. What Cade realized, however, was that sometimes a solution is better than a product.

Some companies would rather spend a couple of million dollars to solve their problem than a few thousand and still have to figure out if it was going to solve their problem. In this instance, our salesman went into the customer and tried to sell them a copy of our software. He also offered them our consulting services if they wanted it, or we could simply train their engineers to do the work. RSS, on the other hand, went into the customer and sold them a solution. For four million dollars, they would put together all of the software and hardware needed to solve their problem. RSS would work with the customer's engineers to get the knowledge from them, but RSS would write all of the software. The customer would then have a solution to their problem. Sure the system was going to have to be a conglomeration of numerous things glued together. In the end, however, it would work, and what did the customer care about how elegant it was. They bought the system from RSS.

I was floored when Cade told me this story, but learned that sometimes companies are like me. I can go to the hardware store a dozen times, buy all of the fixtures and try to figure out how to install a whole new bathroom, or I can just hire a contractor I trust and let him do it. When you're selling software, pretend you're the customer and see what kind of decision they're trying to make. Then you can figure out what to sell them.

The Bad

I have worked with more than those two salesmen listed above, but they're the most memorable for me. Why is it that some of the worst stuff that happens in your life has more viscosity in your memory?

I'll Get Right On It

From the beginning, Whistler was handled mostly as an internal project within the Dylan International Corporation and Bainey Systems division. We started out in a conference room, albeit a nice one with a nice view, before getting our office space set up. Our initial task was to get software working for the internal divisions of the company. However, the longer term goal was to sell externally.

About a year into our development, we had a highly functional system that was being used by a couple of internal divisions. Then, we attended our first trade show as a vendor. Since we didn't have any real sales or marketing people, the developers went to the show and talked to customers. The philosophy behind this was: who better than the developers of the product to sell the product? Well, just about anybody as you'll soon see.

Before we went to the show we had one of the Bainey Salesmen, Kip Willingham, come down to our office to give us a quick training class in how to be salesmen. I know I speak for all of the developers when I say that I was thrilled to be doing this. Here I was going to learn in an afternoon something in which I had no interest, inclination, or talent. We gathered in our conference room and listened to Kip try to tell us what we needed to do. It was a long time ago, but I remember this one snippet of the conversation. Kip had just gone over something presumably important and my manager, Bob Cole, reflected what Kip said, "So first you get your G2."

I sat perplexed for a minute before asking politely, "What the hell is G2?"

"Oh, sorry, it means 'information'," replied Kip.

The rest of the training went pretty much like that exchange and I left the session feeling well armed for my career as a salesman.

After we got home from the trade show Bob divided up the list of leads and handed a batch to each of the developers. He asked us to call the people on the list and try to sell them the software. Did I mention that the software we were selling cost $65,000 and ran on hardware that cost $40,000 per machine? That list went right on the bottom of all the other work I had piled up on my desk. I'm sure that the few days I spent on the phone would have netted the same amount of sales.

I probably don't need to point this out, but I will anyway. Software developers are excellent resources for sales, but are usually poor salespeople. If a salesperson has a question about how the software might help a particular customer solve a particular problem, then pick up the phone. Asking your developers to be salespeople is not a good idea. They have no interest in doing this or they wouldn't be writing software in the first place, they'd be selling it.

How to Reopen the Deal

At Whistler, we almost always competed with ICON for every sale. When two salesmen, Rafe Bronze and Abe Bandon, left ICON we immediately jumped at the opportunity to hire them. One day, when I arrived at the office, there they were. I introduced myself and we exchanged pleasantries and got to the topic of our system versus ICON's. I knew that ICON had recently come out with a surface modeling package that we hadn't even thought about yet. One of these salesman, Rafe Bronze, said, "We're going to need to develop a surface package. We'd like to see it NURBS-based."

I knew that ICON's surfacing package was based on NURBS (non-uniform rational b-splines), but didn't think that these salesmen could tell the difference between NURBS and their elbows. Yes, there was a bit of foreshadowing there. Also, after that day, nobody ever heard from Abe again. He never showed up for work.

Rafe would tell us about numerous deals he was putting together that were potentially worth millions of dollars, but never seemed to be able to close the deals.

On one sales call, our marketing manager, Drew Bergman, went along with him. The sales presentation went very well. The customer was ready to buy. Rafe excused himself to go to the bathroom. Drew remained and the customer asked about how to purchase the software and the possible hardware configurations. When Rafe returned from the bathroom, he sat down and said to the customer, "Well, I guess we ought to get you guys a trial version of the software."

The customer replied, "Oh, I didn't realize that was an option. Okay, let's do that."

Drew slumped in his chair and fumed.

On a personal note, I'm not in favor of selling people something they don't really need, but I know it happens every day, mostly on a smaller scale. This customer could have used the software and they would have benefited from it. There's a fundamental sales strategy that every salesman either knows or should know: try to close the deal. You can fall back on other options, but first, ask the question, "Would you like to buy this?"

Training! We Don't Need No Stinking Training!

Whenever Whistler would hire a salesman, he would come to the next training class. I would occasionally teach the training class or maybe give a lecture on one of my areas of expertise. It would never cease to amaze me that by the third day, all but the occasional salesman were no longer in the class. "I don't need to know how it works to sell it," they would universally say. These people didn't realize what they were in for. If they couldn't survive a week of training, how could they empathize with what they were going to ask the customer to do? These guys were always the ones that said, "Sure the software can do that," even when it couldn't. They never sold anything and were usually gone in a few months.

I'm a firm believer in knowing your product(s) well. If you're going to sell something, you should understand it as well as you can. You'll come across to the customer as more knowledgeable and therefore trustworthy.

I'll Take the High Road and You Take the Low Road and I'll Make the Sale Before Ye

ICON's salesmen were very good at making sales. It always seemed like we were losing to them, even when our software was better suited to the job at hand. The thing was, we were always the choice of the engineers who would have to use the product, while ICON was always the choice of the decision makers. It turns out that our salesmen never aimed at the right place in the company. While we were making the developers happy, they were offering the upper level managers positions of importance in the ICON User's Group which meant occasional junkets to nice destinations for their meetings. If you don't have to actually use the product yourself, you're more likely to pay attention to the folks who are schmoozing with you. Make sure your aim is correct.

The Price is Wrong

While at Ottobon, we started work on a product for architects. Harry Feldman had started the project while investigating the needs of the architectural software market. This was a fairly small group attacking the problem and we were left alone by most of the rest of the company. The closest competition to our product was selling for $495 and did some interesting stuff. Our product attacked the problem space differently and had different functionality. Some of what we could do was better than the competition; some of it just wasn't there yet.

At Ottobon, however, when you were ready to sell the software, it went through a group called the "pricing committee." You could recommend a price point for the software, but the decision was ultimately theirs. We suggested a retail price of $295. But, this company usually sold software in the $3000 range, with only a few products below $1000, most of which

104

didn't sell very well. The committee ultimately priced the product at $895. Although the product was well received and well reviewed by the media, it was simply too expensive for what it did. We had hoped that a low price would let architects make a quick purchase decision and at $200 to $300, you can do that. Once you get above the $500 mark, you're talking about an investment and need to decide if the product is really right for you. In the end, we didn't sell many copies and the project was cancelled. Although not entirely to blame for the product's failure, the price was wrong.

The Arguly

The What?

At Whistler, I worked with a guy from Taiwan named Joe Chan. His English was pretty good, but his pronunciation was a bit off at times. I once got an email from him that contained the word "arguly." Curious, I went to talk to him and asked him what the word meant. He said it out loud for me and it sounded like "ahgully," which was how he pronounced the word "ugly." This hasn't anything to do with the ugliest sales things I've seen, but it's my favorite story about Joe and I still use his pronunciation frequently. Yes, this is a complete non sequitur.

It Could Fall Off? Really?

While we were competing with ICON for a major contract in England, the customer started asking us questions regarding our system's performance. We told them about our capabilities and our side-by-side tests with ICON's software. It finally came to light that one of ICON's salesmen claimed that our software wasn't designed to be used with very large models.

In reality, our system was very good with large models. Additionally, while the ICON system may have been designed for use with large models, their memory management support wasn't. At the time, both systems used LISP as a programming language. LISP uses automatic memory management, which is performed by a "garbage collector." But we used different LISP vendors and they had different underlying technology. At that time it meant that every so often, your application might stop while memory was examined for possible reuse. Our garbage collector was much faster than ICON's. Theirs was so slow, in fact, that it would usually lock up the application for about an hour! Their customers quickly figured out that it was faster to kill the application and start it back up again, rather than to wait. Talk about performance killers.

By this time, I'd grown weary of ICON's stone-throwing routines during sales competition and one day, to let off steam, I made a joke about the whole thing. My story involved the ICON salesmen telling the customer that continued use of Whistler's product would cause "certain side-effects", but you only have to reboot *our* system.

Personally, I don't like trash talking the competition with customers. Every system is going to have pros and cons, better and worse functionality than the competition. I think sales people should sell the good stuff they have and ask themselves how much their integrity is worth? As a consumer, and we're all consumers, ask yourself if the trash talking salesman is going to support you when you have a problem. Who would you rather have on your side?

Ouch! A Hit Below the Belt

Since our goal at Whistler was to compete with ICON, we had similar functionality and naming conventions. In a few months, we were able to solve many of the same problems that they could. At one point a customer told us that an ICON salesman had told them that Whistler had found the ICON source code on a computer at another division of Dylan International. They said that Whistler had stolen it, and were passing it off as their own. We didn't get the sale, but I really don't know if this had anything to do with it.

Words can't express how I felt when I heard this. Well, they can, but I can't reprint them here. In my opinion this kind of sales tactic is disgusting, disgraceful, and dishonest. You can try to outsell the software that I write, but lying about it is hitting below the belt. Years later when my company was purchased by ICON, I had little desire to work for them. I felt that their sales tactics were reflective of the whole company.

Discussion and Thought Questions

1. In your career, you will have opportunities to sell. It could be that you're even selling yourself to a prospective employer or selling yourself for a promotion or raise. How will you "close the deal" in these situations?

2. Have there been situations where you've dealt with a sales bully? Was he trying to sell you a car, computer, software, or even vinyl windows for your house? In the short term these techniques can be effective, but they tend to work poorly in building long term relationships with customers.

Chapter 10: To Boss or Not To Boss – Management

So much of what we call management consists in making it difficult for people to work.

- Peter F. Drucker

Management is a funny thing. Good management can make all the difference in your company and so can bad management. There's a myth that managers are in their jobs because they have all the knowledge and answers. Some of you reading this are laughing right now, either because you used to think this or can't believe that I was once that naïve. You haven't heard this myth? Well, maybe not. This is the way I felt about managers when I started working, though I don't know where I came up with it. I guess I just figured that you were a manager because you knew that kind of stuff, just like I was a programmer because I knew *that* kind of stuff. It wasn't too long before I figured out that I was dead wrong - especially after I became a manager myself.

The Ladder of Babel

Management is an interesting label, used to describe just about anyone who has supervisory responsibility for other people, but this is not always the case. You'll meet dozens of people in your career with the word "manager" in their title who don't manage people per-se.

There's nothing more obvious than the management chain in a company. Many managers simply manage other managers. When you look at things that way, you start to realize that the higher up the ladder the manager, the less they are likely to know anything about the details of what you do and vice versa. I'm not saying that these people aren't technically competent. Many of them are, or at least were when they were worker bees, but they've started working at more abstract levels now. Conversations and company meetings are interesting because of the wide gap in knowledge and focus on different aspects of the work involved in running the company.

You might reasonably expect that a first line manager who has engineers working for him will have technical knowledge, but even that's not always the case. Many managers are simply organizers of work and connectors of people, with little knowledge of your daily work. This isn't necessarily bad either, but it is something to be aware of.

In communicating with people higher up the management chain, you need to generalize the kinds of things you say and the way that you say them. They usually don't understand the technical details of what you're doing as they focus on things at the corporate level, like financial concerns, the direction and strategy for the company, corporate partnerships, embezzlement, and packing up their golden parachutes. All right, I'm being a bit flippant about the last two items, but the last one is very common, actually, and since I've never been in a position to pack one, I'm not qualified to go into any detail about it.

Conversely, whenever you go to a company meeting and the CEO or President starts talking, you'll probably understand about half of what they have to say. The other half will be about corporate this and financial that — stuff you might actually care about, but simply don't have the background to understand. (This is why many CEOs come from the bean-counting side of the world.) Of the half that you understand, about half will actually make sense to you. The other part will sound like double speak and fuzzy logic. For example, your CEO might say, "We expect that sales will rebound in the next quarter when we release our next suite of products. We are also hopeful that the softening of the construction market will not completely evaporate the seeds we've planted in the corresponding market spaces." The first part sounds pretty straightforward, but the second part is probably just saying, "Of course, we don't really have a clue what sales are going to do, but if they nosedive, don't say we didn't warn everybody right here in black in white. And, by the way, it's not our fault, either. So keep those stock options coming and keep my corporate jet fueled."

As you go higher on the corporate ladder, you start to have less technical and more strategic responsibilities. Instead of thinking about code, schedules, and personnel, you start thinking more about what direction the product(s) should go, how to open up new markets for your product(s) and what new product(s) you should build. As this has a big impact on your company as a whole, people in these positions get paid more and have a bigger pot of potential money-making perks, like stock options and bonuses.

For each step up the management ladder, it's not uncommon to see an increase in salary of 25%. The stock options, however, may go up by 100% or more. At one company I worked for, I was given stock options. They were fairly generous, usually on the order of 500 to 1000 shares every year or so. After a few years, they were worth a good sum of money – I can't complain. However, the CEO of the company would cash in his stock options in increments of 50,000 shares, usually on a bi-monthly basis. The higher you go, the better the perks.

An Army of One

Project managers and marketing managers are usually managers of things, not people. I don't mean this in a derogatory sense at all; it's just usually what they do.

Project managers are responsible for the running of the entire project. They usually track the master schedule, organize meetings for people to communicate cross-team issues, help track down cross-team issues, and generally bug the heck out of everyone else to get their jobs done. They make sure that the software is on schedule, the marketing campaign will be ready for the big release, sales is getting their information on what features will be in the actual product, quality assurance will be done testing, documentation will be printed, and production will be ready to turn the software into CDs (if you ship CDs anymore). A good project manager can really help keep all of the other players in sync and pick up the balls that occasionally get dropped on a project. Yet, they produce nothing of permanence on the project. Once the software is released, they can throw away all of their schedules, to do lists, and action items, and nobody will miss them. However, their role in the support of your project can be invaluable. Give your project manager a hug today.

Marketing managers are a mixed bag of people managers and thing managers. For example, if you read the chapter on marketing, you know about the guy who managed a document. Whether you are a manager of people or just a marketing person trying to do a particular job, you probably have the word manager at the end of your title. I think it's a prestige thing in marketing, kind of like being a producer in television. Have you noticed that all of the people who used to be listed in the credits at the end of a television show are now listed at the bottom of the screen starting at the beginning of the show? The list goes on for about ten minutes and will soon cover the entire duration of the program. The two people who used to have the title "Executive Producer" and "Producer" (there really are only two of them) will soon be named "Super Senior Executive Five Star Producer" and "Senior Masterful Producing Producer." Everyone else who just had normal jobs will soon be producers, including the woman who picks up the donuts in the morning, now the "Toroidal Glugocular Carbohydrate Procurement Producer." The marketing folks have already been there for years. Do not let yourself be impressed by titles. Ask these people what they actually do and you'll get a better sense that they're usually worker bees just like you, but with a more pretentious title.

Occasionally, software folks get creative in a similar fashion and create titles for themselves such as "Guru of GUI", "Sultan of Semicolons", and "Duke of Data Structures". Fortunately these are mostly internal names not seen by the public. Back when *NYPD Blue* was still on television, I noticed that everyone they interviewed had a "street name". Detective Sipowicz would interview some snitch who would say, "Well, his name is Arnie Rosenblatt, but he goes by the name of Snake." I thought we should do the same thing at work, "My name is Bill Myers, but I program under the name of Razor." I think I forgot about the whole thing when I got distracted by being called "bill dot myers", which is unfortunately much less cool than "Razor".

Software Management

Now that we've talked a bit about upper management and managers who don't manage anyone at all, let's get to software management.

Dr. Rorschach to the Rescue

Just as you may take a test during a job interview as a programmer, you may also be asked to take a test for a management position. Management tests tend to be more about logic and decision-making. I've personally taken a couple of different kinds of tests like this, one administered by a company who used psychologists to determine your suitability for management, the other was an in-house test aimed more at logic and decisions.

What Does Dr. Rorschach Know Anyway?

Although these tests exist, it is far more common for people to move into management based on their own performance as an engineer. On the plus side, the new manager is technically competent; on the minus side, there's a lot to management that has nothing to do with technical competence.

Bob was technically competent and eventually given a management position based on his abilities. His people appreciated his ability to help them solve problems, design systems, understand their roadblocks and delays, and share in their elegant solutions. The managerial aspects of the job were much more difficult (and much less interesting), but his boss was supportive and helpful with these tasks. Although his company had training classes for some specific managerial responsibilities, it didn't have a real program which covered the gamut of what needed to be done and how to best do it. I suspect that this is a common problem.

Bob was truly geared for and gifted to be a technical manager, but was not a great organizational manager and this part of the job was much harder. It really is a skill set all its own and before you decide whether to take a management job, you should get a thorough understanding of the expectations of the position.

Boymeat Swirled

At one job, Bob got a new manager who had different expectations of what a manager should do, and Bob had difficulty adjusting. He was still very technically minded and was focused on those aspects of his work. However, in his new situation, there was a greater need for inter-group communication, coordination, and scheduling, which were not his strong suits.

To make things more difficult, his manager had other products and groups to manage and didn't keep his eye on Bob's product very closely, causing him to be frequently surprised at decisions and events. Towards the end of the development cycle of a new product, Bob informed his manager that they were going to miss their code complete date. Unbeknownst to Bob, missing this date could have caused the company to lose millions of dollars in revenue.

After the release of the product, on time, but after four months of night and weekend work, he asked Bob to return to software development work, which he happily did.

As you can see, changing expectations, responsibilities, and managers can have a huge affect on your performance. In any new situation, be sure to establish what is expected of you. If it doesn't fit you well, think about making a change of some sort – a transfer, a shift in responsibilities, or a return to pure development may work better for you in the long run.

The Search for Spock

Hiring software managers from outside your company is a tough job. They will usually not have the same technical background or insight as the people they will manage. As they are looking for a management position, they will tend to be people who like the true management aspect of their work and this can seem strange to their prospective developers.

At one point, my group needed to hire a new development manager. We interviewed two guys who seemed well suited to the task. One was Sam Mercer, who seemed like a very nice guy with a wealth of management experience. The other was Igor, a somewhat humorless man who seemed like he would do the job well, but might be hard to work with and for. The management team voted for Igor; the software developers voted for Sam. One of the developers felt that although he liked Sam better, Igor might be better for us by whipping us into shape. I got the distinct impression that the management team felt the same way, as they believed that the software engineers were too soft and lazy and needed some whipping. Our director, Jack, settled the dispute by hiring Sam, whom he felt was much more qualified and apt to do a better job. The developers were happy - for about three or four months.

It took about that long to find out that Sam couldn't communicate very well. In our team meetings, he would tell us what he wanted in elliptical descriptions that we would spend ten minutes of questioning trying to decipher. He had no technical knowledge whatsoever, which the developers found hard to identify with as they were accustomed to having this in a manager. And even though there were senior technical members of the team and Jack wanted to have technical leadership for technical issues and organizational leadership for a manager, people had a hard time not getting both from the same person. Without a single go-to person for technical decisions, these things became a committee issue. Although we all got along well, a single technical lead that had the final say definitely would have helped.

It also took about that long to find out that Sam was incapable of taking a true leadership role. He couldn't make a decision without worrying that Jack or one of the other managers would overrule him. He had lost his opportunity to earn the respect of his team. Grumblings were eventually passed on to the Human Resources representative, who passed our concerns to Jack. When Jack finally visited the office (he was based in California while we were in New York), we tried to convey to him how we felt about our new manager. Have you ever noticed that what sounds so bad when you talk among your colleagues doesn't have the same impact when you report it to your manager? We had the same experience. Every complaint sounded like a petty thing, but the sum total was greater than its parts. Nonetheless, Jack maintained his support for Sam and life went on. To his credit, Sam confronted the group in our next meeting and asked us to lay out our concerns. He was very open and listened well. It actually gave him a temporary notch up on the totem pole in our book.

Unfortunately, he didn't follow through on the things he said he would do for our team. He had promised to teach the group UML (Unified Modeling Language), but kept hedging on actually doing it. He had also promised guidance on a new software development process, but that was not forthcoming either. The team also wondered about the amount of contribution he was making when his main goal for the day was to "craft an email".

Things over the next few months didn't really improve. In his first release of the software as manager, he allowed the team to reach its code complete milestone on time. Unfortunately, there were pieces that weren't complete, but he didn't want to say that we missed the deadline. To be fair, this is sometimes a dicey decision, but after years of experience, you learn that it's better in the long run to simply admit that you missed the first deadline than to pretend things are great and start missing the later ones.

The next time Jack came to visit, he called another group meeting. He said that although we weren't really happy with

Sam, at least it felt like this release was going better than the last one. One of the team, Connie, actually spoke up and said that it really wasn't any better. We had allowed a deadline to pass that we really had missed without actually recognizing it. The team spent the next four months working nights and weekends to finish the release.

Hindsight is the Better Part of Valor

Sorry, I have a habit of mixing metaphors. Almost every experience gives you an opportunity to learn something. The lesson may be about yourself or someone else. After some bad experiences, it's easy to make excuses or point the finger at another person. In truth, the blame can often be spread around, but the percentage of the blame isn't nearly as important as the acceptance of some of it.

As with any position you take in software, know what's expected of you and if you're the manager, tell your people what's expected of them.

I believe that Jack should have spent more time focusing on what was going on in his development organizations. Sam would have been more effective overall if he had followed through with what he promised his development group and earned their respect. I also feel that learning more about the software would have increased his ability to communicate the group's accomplishments and challenges more effectively. When Bob got a new manager, he should have listened more carefully to his new set of expectations. Perhaps he could have avoided his almost disastrous situation with better communication.

In my career, I've learned so much from the mistakes I've made that you would think I should be perfect by now. I can just hear the laughter from my friends, family, and colleagues from all across the country at the very thought of it.

Great Expectations

One of my favorite books on software development is *Rapid Development*. In it, there are listed numerous classic mistakes in trying to shorten your development cycle. You have probably already heard how adding developers to a late project makes it later. This, of course, can depend on whom you add. If you add someone who you recently took off the project or someone who has specialized knowledge of some aspect of the project and won't need much ramp up time, you might actually help. Usually this isn't the case. The new person needs to ask questions and the other engineers are slowed down bringing the new person up to speed. The new person also breaks the code or the build by not being familiar with the code or the code check-in procedures. If you want your project to come in later, go ahead and add some more people. If you really want to help, try to remove obstacles instead. Reduce meetings rather than have a daily meeting to find out how to get to the finish line faster. Bring in food, offer to run errands, or remove time wasting processes.

Now back to the topic at hand. My favorite classic mistake, which many managers don't know is a mistake, is to create unrealistic expectations. How do you do this? The most common way is to tell developers that their schedule estimates are either too long or that they need to be done in much less time. In the "How to Lose Millions of Dollars" chapter, I told you about Hal Samson, who gave us 5 months to complete 11 months of work and you saw how well that worked.

At Ottobon, at the end of one release, we were given two weeks to fix 150 bugs. Developers look at ploys like this and think that the managers are just idiots. They sit around for two hours and bitch about the impossibility of achieving the impossible. Then they ignore the very sense of urgency you are trying to create because they know that it's all just a bunch of hooey.

Wait. This isn't what you were trying to have happen? Bummer, that's what really happens. If you want your people to rally, work hard, be loyal, and give you their best, then you have to do the same as their manager. Asking for a stretch is one thing. Asking the impossible is just that and developers see right through it.

What's in a Name?

What is a manager? You may have noticed that there have been a number of people in different positions and with different responsibilities with the word "manager" in their title. I believe that this is a little easier to define in terms of software engineering. There are two main areas of software management, technical and organizational. By the way, I've read numerous books on management in general and never gotten a good understanding of all of the activities you might need to perform. I *have* read some good books on the leadership aspect of management and the different styles of management.

I'll start with the technical as that's the easiest to understand and perform if you're a software engineer already. The usual path for becoming a manager is through achievement in engineering. If your focus will be on technical leadership, then this is a great transformation possibility. As a technical manager, your focus will change from solving each individual problem, designing code, and writing code to becoming more of a consultant. You'll want to review your team's designs and code, be available to answer questions and address problems, and direct the team's activities. You don't have to poke your nose into everything, but will want to provide an example of taking responsibility for what goes on and have everyone in your group share that responsibility. I'm not saying that every member of your team needs to know how to do everything. I am saying that you want your team to know that you, the manager, can't do everything either. If they see a problem coming up, they should tell you and hopefully have some ideas on how to solve it rather than just dumping it all on you. Once your team learns to trust that you're not going to freak out at losing control of all the strings that make your team move like a well-rehearsed marionette show, you may not need to confront problems as frequently because your people will simply solve the problems as they arise. As a technical manager, you don't need to have all of the answers to earn respect. You do need to have a clue, however. If you're new to the group, you'll want to learn how things work as quickly as possible so that you can see the big picture properly. This is the one thing that you must keep in mind. Your job is not just to see the details, but to piece together the parts.

The organizational manager is a more difficult transformation to make for most software engineers. The main reason for this is that your job will begin to entail tasks with which you have less experience. Here's a partial list of your possible responsibilities:

1. Choosing a process.

2. Software estimation

3. Initial scheduling and schedule maintenance

4. Task and project assignment

5. Milestone setting

6. Coordination with other teams

7. Coordination within your team

8. Communication of your group's activities

9. Writing performance reviews

10. Planning and evaluating salary and bonuses

11. Interviewing candidates

12. Dealing with personal and personnel problems

13. Hardware and software requirements and purchasing

14. Giving presentations

15. Meeting with upper management

16. Meeting with customers

17. Budgeting

18. Clairvoyance

As you can see from this list, most of it is non-technical work. You've probably performed some aspects of these tasks, e.g. estimating the time to complete a project, but may have been able to simply report this information to your manager and then gone back to what you were doing ten minutes ago, just before she asked for your estimate. As the manager, you'll now need to take such well thought out and researched information and turn it into something that upper management will try to cast in stone as if there were some absolute truth to it.

If you read the list carefully, you also noticed the last item, clairvoyance. This is difficult to achieve, but is expected of you. I recommend that you invest in both a Ouija board and a high quality set of tarot cards. If there's room in your budget for a bona fide psychic or you have one on your team, that's even better. I'm only half joking about it, actually. One thing that you can do to attempt clairvoyance is to simply imagine what can go wrong. Some people classify this task as "risk management". You note all of the things that can go wrong and develop a plan to deal with all of the items on the list.

Your company may provide training classes in some of these tasks. I took a class in scheduling, for example. I can tell you that this is still a dark art, rather than a science. You'll be taught that you can break down all of the work into simple tasks that can be more easily estimated, but some of your developers will be better at providing useful information about this than others. One of my best developers provided me with the most useless task breakdowns you can imagine. For example, for the new copy and paste functionality, I would get three tasks: design classes – 2 days, write classes – 10 days, test classes – 1 day. If the classes had already been designed, which they should have been for a better estimate, I would get two tasks: implement classes – 12.5 days, test classes – 1 day. As you might guess, having other developers try to see if they agreed with these estimates or might provide more insight was useless as well. If you insist that your developers do some prototyping and really map out the work involved, this will be much more accurate. When you try to schedule all of your tasks, make sure that an appropriate amount of slush is added to the time given. Most developers don't get to code for eight solid hours a day. Between meetings, chatting at the coffee machine, helping a colleague, and mindless web surfing, you may only get 4 to 6 hours of actual coding work in a day.

While I'm on the subject, let me just touch on this for a minute: the more frequently a developer has to switch tasks, the less productive he will be. If you're going to schedule meetings for your team, try to do them around known breaks in work. For example, let's say that your team tends to show up at 9AM, break for lunch at noon, and go home around 6PM. Schedule meetings at 9:15 (allows them to grab some coffee and quickly check their email), 11:30 (they'll just go to lunch afterwards), or 1PM (they'll get back from lunch and head into the meeting, although they may also doze off if the meeting is too long and dull). If you schedule the meeting mid-morning or mid-afternoon, they'll tend to plan their day around the interruption. All it takes is one mid-morning and one mid-afternoon meeting to kill a developer's whole day. It's very difficult to keep booting up their brains for coding when they know that they won't have very long to work before the next meeting.

Some of the tasks I've listed above are related, but a good management training program should include at least an introductory class in the first twelve items, although you may disagree with which ones are most important. Unfortunately, most of the things on this list are more art than science. You can try to apply logic and mathematics to some of it, thus creating SWAGs (scientific wild ass guesses), but it's still an art. I haven't found a good source of information on all of these requirements yet. Maybe I'll do some research on this and write one for my next book. Hmm…

As the state of the art is today, you'll have to rely on your best guesses, a training class in a few of the topics, and maybe a good mentor. I wish I could say more, but the topic is so big, it would require a book or two on its own. My one sage word of advice is to establish as best as possible what is expected of you and by you. It's a bit of covering your ass, yes, but failing to do so can only lead to future difficulties. If you're the head coach of a football team that has had a winning season for 10 years in a row, but all of your veterans have retired and you've got a team full of rookies, it would be a good idea to let everyone know that this is a rebuilding year and that great things may be ahead, but it will take time. Set people's expectations realistically and then try your best to delight them.

Herding _____ (your animal goes here)

I'm not going to talk too much about this topic. If you're familiar with software engineers, or are one, then you've probably heard the expression that managing a group of them is like herding cats. In other words, it ain't easy.

Most software engineers don't wish to be cats; it's just their nature and the nature of the profession. One developer Bob had working for him was highly prone to this and developed a bad reputation for always being behind schedule. Bob worked with him more closely to try and correct this by checking in with him and keeping him more focused on his own code. Yes, the others in the group would have to write their own code to solve their problems, but at least Bob was able to track his progress more accurately and his reputation was bolstered.

His failure to meet his schedule was also detracting from Bob's managerial reputation as well. Everyone would look at Bob's development schedule and notice that he was behind. You can see how this kind of thing can snowball.

As manager, your job is to keep the cats walking in the same direction and minimizing the off-track movement, or wandercoding (See the section on Wandercoding in Chapter 11), as much as possible.

What the Hell is Going on Here?

In my opinion, the most important thing you can do as a manager is to simply know what's going on. You should talk to your people regularly and not just rely on their weekly status reports or a weekly status meeting. You should talk to your colleagues and find out what they're doing. Of course, you should talk to your manager and find out what he or she wants and what he or she is doing.

Since communication is such a big part of management, having knowledge of what's going on is invaluable. You'll be able to make connections between developers who are both thinking about solving the same problem or perhaps one of them just solved it, but the other doesn't know it yet. When you run into your boss in the hallway and he asks you how Calvin is coming along with the transmogrification module, you'll be able to tell him.

You'll make decisions that are more informed, be surprised less often, and be more proactive when you know what's going on. Pick up the phone, walk over to a cube or office, or meet for lunch. Pick one of the above.

Weakly Meeting

In my whole career, I have always hated the weekly status meeting. They have run the gamut from two-hour bitch-fests to filling out a schedule while everyone else sat and watched until it was their turn. Your people's time would be much better spent by writing up a summary of their week that you put together into a report for your manager and your subordinates. If you must meet every week, try to make it a downward communication vehicle where you tell your people what's going on. You can then ask if anyone has anything of interest that they'd like to report for the rest of the crew to hear. Keep these meetings short and sweet and your folks won't dread them.

At one point, Bob's manager wanted him to hold weekly meetings with his group. He knew that as soon as he sent out a meeting request with a regular time and location that he would hear a collective groan. Instead, he simply picked a random time and location for a meeting once a week. One week, he would schedule a conference room for 9:15AM on Monday. The next week, on Tuesday morning, he sent out a note saying that his group would simply pull their chairs around in the common space between the cubicles. They met every week this way, but since most of the communication came from Bob and the times seemed so random, nobody was the wiser.

What Smells in Here?

When you walk into a room, you sometimes ask yourself, "What smells in here?" The same thing can happen in your company or organization. Why is morale so low? Why does everyone work at home when they don't live that far away from the office? Do they like the peace and quiet of their home office or hate their workplace, colleagues, or managers? Why is turnover so high? Why is productivity or quality so low?

It could be the workers or the management and it can be hard to tell which one is really the problem. If you really have a bunch of incompetent software developers, then that may be the problem. I'm not one to point fingers, but in my experience, I've never seen a group of developers that can't get a job done when they have competent management. Most of the time, even without competent management, they've found a way to make the software work and get their job done. Therefore, my conclusion is usually that you have a management issue. It may not always be bad management, but perhaps just a mismatch of styles with the people being managed.

One company in town has a reputation for simply being a horrible place to work. They are often noted for having low pay and difficult people to work for. Low pay is more easily overcome as most people are happy in a job where they feel satisfied with what they're doing and who they work with and for. I've talked to people who work there and used to work there. I have no desire to apply for a job there. Would you?

Dave, a former colleague, told me that his manager, Phil, had called him a liar in a meeting. He said that Phil was already a pain to work for, but when that happened, and happened in front of other people from other teams in the company, he decided that he would begin planning his exit from the company. When Phil did it again in another meeting, it didn't take long for Dave to follow through, more quickly than he actually wanted to leave. He simply wasn't going to take any more. Phil was able to get results from his team, but there wasn't a lot of joy going on at work. His team lacked enthusiasm and a sense of teamwork and loyalty. While the work got done, Bill's team was destined to undergo a lot of turnover.

If you walk into your office and it smells of bad management and you have the power to do something about it, don't just assume the problem will go away. Your employees may not be leaving, but they aren't producing what they could.

Or You'll Go to Bed Without Any Dinner

One thing that software developers hate (and I mean really hate) is being threatened. While they respond well to words of encouragement, they don't respond well to yelling or threats. You may want to tell your crew that they'd better fix every damn bug in the system by Friday or they'll be working over the weekend, but resist the temptation to make it sound harsh. If you say, "I know this stinks, but we need to have all the bugs fixed by Monday and I know we'd like to have a nice weekend. Let's do this by Friday," you'll get a much better result. You're dealing with professionals who are trying to do their best. Unfortunately, software development isn't like football, where you can just try harder to fix the bugs or write the code faster.

During one release cycle, the team I was on ran behind schedule and was in danger of missing our ship date. My boss and his boss, Hank, both came out for a visit. They wanted to address the team as they often did. I warned them ahead of time that threatening the team would not go over well. I don't know if it was their intent or just the words they chose, but the team took their words as a threat. After the meeting, everybody knew what needed to be done, but morale was in the pits for months.

Subtlety is key here. Even the way that you say something can turn a benign message into a dire one. During a previous project, the same manager, Hank, had come for a visit. Some of the developers were working on fixing bugs for another product, but wanted to start working on the new product. They asked Hank when this would happen. Hank replied, "You don't get to work on the new product until you finish what you're already fixing."

This seemed like a reasonable answer to me, but some of the developers thought it sounded threatening. They felt that Hank was saying that they hadn't proven they were worthy of working on the new product yet, or some other horrible suggestion. I didn't get that impression, but it didn't really matter because some people did. See how easy it is to send morale downhill?

In my research, I have found numerous articles about the positive correlation between high morale and high productivity. I have not been able to find a positive correlation between high productivity and fear. You do the math, so to speak.

Successor success

At one job, I was given the amusing task of choosing a successor when and if I was no longer the manager of the group. I had one person in my group of ten who would have made a good manager. However, she had no interest whatsoever in going into management. The very idea made her shiver and that was about the end of the conversation. She was smart. She knew what a thankless, painful, time-engulfing job I had and she wasn't even going to think about taking it.

This is a common reaction among software engineers. The qualities that make developers good at what they do, namely a desire to design, write, and debug code, much of which is a solitary, introspective job, are polar opposites of the qualities that are needed for management. Unfortunately, this makes good software development managers hard to find.

Discussion and Thought Questions

1. Are you interested in management? What aspects do you find most intriguing?

2. If you're a manager, what style of management do you use? Do your engineers respect you? If so, what do they respect you for? Is it your leadership, technical expertise, organization, or the fact that you buy the beer every Friday?

3. If you're a manager, how do you treat your employees? Do you threaten them frequently? Do you provide motivation?

Chapter 11: They Come in All Shapes and Sizes – Software Engineers

I've classified all of your bugs into three categories: lethal, boneheaded, and vexing.

- Scott Adams in "Dilbert"

Unlike the old stereotypes about computer geeks with taped-together eyeglasses and pocket protectors, software engineers are a wide-ranging bunch of people and personalities. Sure there are geeks, but for the most part if you were to talk to a variety of the people in the business and wouldn't know what they did for a living, you might never guess.

One from column A, Two from column B

Like the categories of software bugs, most software engineers fit into a set of categories as well. That's not to say that everyone fits into these or that this is an exhaustive list, but there are some stereotypical classes nonetheless. If you're already a software engineer, then you might see yourself or one of your colleagues in one of these descriptions. More likely, you'll see a bit of yourself in a few of them.

Penalty on Number 86 – Five Minutes for Uselessness

One day my manager referred to a guy in the home office as a hockey puck so I asked him what it meant. He replied that it was when you could replace the programmer with a hockey puck and didn't notice the difference. Ouch!

Then there was the guy from Ottobon's newly opened India office, Pradeep. He and his manager came over to the New York office for a couple of weeks to help him get up to speed. We were giving him some new printing functionality to work on. The two worst things you can give someone to work on in a graphical application are printing and text. If your boss offers you a great opportunity to pick up a project on either of these two topics run away fast. If you don't understand why, go ahead and accept the assignment; you'll understand when you're done. Apparently, management felt that the best thing to do with the printing code was to ship it overseas as nobody in the U.S. wanted to deal with it. Pradeep had everyone in the development group meet with him in the conference room and describe the workings of a part of the software that they understood best. Everyone gave him their best explanation of the things that they knew about, but almost none of it had to do with printing.

He went home and began working on his new functionality. After a few weeks, he emailed a colleague, Connie, and asked a few questions. He talked about how he was going to have to rewrite this piece of code and add that code to make things work properly. Her reply was that his assumptions were right on the money. Well, months went by and code wasn't being checked into the system. This caused some concern, but his manager had apparently been hounding him to check in his code and was assured that it was forthcoming, but wasn't quite ready yet. As the code complete deadline neared, the code still wasn't in. On Jack's (the director of engineering) next visit to India, he sat down with Pradeep and got the same story. Finally, Jack asked if there really was any code to check in. Pradeep replied that no, there wasn't. He was ashamed, but he had been unable to figure out what to do and how to do it. He left the company. Now, his colleagues in India were not too happy that the incident with Pradeep was going to start our relationship with them on the wrong foot and volunteered to do the work. They worked long hours, asked lots of questions and got the code done. It was late, but it worked.

Pradeep was probably a reasonably intelligent guy who could have done the work, but had too much pride to admit that he needed help and didn't know what was going on. The lesson here is that even though you may not be worthless, if you don't produce anything usable, in the end, you're still a hockey puck. If you have a colleague who has an excuse for everything and doesn't produce what needs to get done, you may have one on your hands. Keep in mind that there's a big difference between dropping the ball on something and being useless. Dropping a ball happens to everyone occasionally.

The Bonehead

Everybody knows one of these. He's the guy who you just know is going to mess up whatever he's given. There are several degrees of boneheadedness, ranging from mild to severe. We all suffer from a mild version from time to time, but the severe ones are harder to tolerate. If your builds are always broken, your code has always been hacked with bad code to handle some exceptional case and it's likely to crash, or the code simply doesn't do anything close to what it's supposed to do, you may have a bonehead on your hands.

At Rocky International there was a guy, Mark, who suffered from serial mild boneheadedness. This isn't as bad as a severe bonehead, but it did require that we all keep our eyes on what he was doing. For example, he was told to implement some new requirements on some functionality originally developed by Bob. Mark went to Bob and asked if he had read the requirements correctly, but Mark didn't want to hear the explanation of the proper implementation. Bob knew Mark would get it wrong and, sure enough, a couple weeks later saw the bug report appear in the system. Bob grabbed the bug and fixed it. If Mark had simply listened to the full explanation in the first place, a lot of wasted time and effort would have been prevented.

The Know-It-All and the Expert

Everyone has dealt with a Know-It-All at one time or another. He has an answer for everything, right or wrong. If he's knowledgeable, almost always right, and is nice about it, then you have an expert, and this is a good thing. However, if the answer is frequently wrong and he's hard to convince otherwise, then he's just a pain in the butt.

Bradley, a former colleague who worked in a remote office, was a Know-It-All. He felt he was a paragon of programming. To be fair, he was good, but far from perfect. He wrote good code as well as horribly inefficient, indecipherable garbage. When anyone in the group checked in code, a document had to be written with an explanation of what code was changed and why (see Dominance and Submission later in the book). This document was emailed to the entire team so everyone could see what files had changed and for what reason. If Bradley thought that it was a particularly good or particularly bad check-in, he would email a reply to the entire group saying so. Why he couldn't just email the person in private was beyond me.

Experts, on the other hand are great to work with. The best of them are still humble, easy to work with, and open to discussion and suggestions. They know their stuff, but still have respect for the other people that they work with, rather than looking down their noses at everyone else. At Ottobon, there was a guy named Arlo, who knew more about his field of expertise (computer graphics) than many people in the world. He gave lectures at conferences, wrote a book, and edited technical papers and magazines – all in addition to getting his work done. He was a pleasure to work with, taught everyone a lot about some of his special knowledge, but also listened to and used some of our crazy suggestions about his area of expertise to solve some of his problems. Good people get recognition without having to broadcast their deeds too much.

The Bottleneck

At Rocky International, there was a woman, Crystal, who was in charge of the product requirements. She had some experience doing software development in the previous release of the product and knew about some of the components. Unfortunately, she wasn't very thorough. When you looked up the list of things that you needed to implement, there was always stuff missing – even things that were common to every feature. Additionally, there were always questionable items on the list. In order to get an answer to a question or to have the requirements modified, you had to write an official action item. These were supposed to be looked at and addressed in a timely basis, i.e. in a few days. Unfortunately, she was always busy with something and these piled up for weeks and even months. As a result, the development team quickly got behind schedule. Every few weeks, she would come in on the weekend or work late and knock off a few dozen action items in a few hours. The next day, she'd relate with pride that she'd come in on Sunday and taken care of forty action items. This was of little consolation when you had already been waiting for ages. Why she couldn't just answer a few each day and keep up a steady flow was both frustrating and perplexing.

Beyond this, many of the action items were brought on by simply not doing a complete job in the first place. If there was a common item missing on your list of things to address, she'd just say that she expected you to catch it and write an action item as she didn't have the time to be thorough the first time because she was too busy. However, this ended up costing not only her time, but everyone else's as well. In the end, instead of just taking the extra ten minutes to check over her work and easily add the features you needed, this is how it would go:

o The developer would look at the feature set.

o The developer would put together a design based on those features.

o The developer would write down the feature numbers in the design.

o The developer would write a document which included the design (and the included feature numbers) as well as a list of the features and the description.

So far, all of this is standard so this doesn't add any time.

o If the developer noticed the missing items, they would have written an action item and that would be included in the design document. This takes a few minutes.

o If the developer didn't notice the missing items, then hopefully someone else who reviewed the document would notice. An informal action item from the meeting would be created to write a formal action item to have the feature assigned to that project. This takes a few minutes.

o Crystal would still have to assign the feature to your project. This only takes a minute, but you'd still have to wait for her to get to it through her long list of other action items. *You'd usually have to wait a few weeks for this.*

o The developer would get the action item back and add the number to the design. A few minutes.

o The developer would add the feature to the design document and include the new feature number from the software design. A few minutes.

o The developer would send the action item to the project manager. A minute.

o The project manager would approve the closure of the action item. A minute.

You can see that this would now involve extra people who would have to review this work to make sure it was complete, taking longer than the initial checking would have done. Of course, this kind of thing creates volumes of electronic paperwork and all of those counts of "a few minutes" could easily add up to an hour or more. The big problem was the frequently inserted weeks of waiting. Nothing stacks up a schedule more than being unable to complete projects due to a Bottleneck.

If you find a Bottleneck at work, they can cause serious problems. If you can't convince them to be thorough or timely, perhaps their management can.

The Purist, the Hacker, and the Pragmatist

Most of the programmers you run into will fall into one of these categories. All of these people produce working code, but it varies widely in quality, maintainability, and the timeliness of its production.

The purist must adhere to every convention. He wants everything laid out perfectly no matter how long it takes. While this is an admirable quality, they often over-apply this, even to small things that should simply be written and revisited later, if necessary. The purist is the most likely to write up a coding style guideline and tick off everyone else with some of the edicts it contains. He is also the most likely to over-design his code. This can be a good quality to have in some people on your team. Purists keep the other programmers from being too sloppy. The Purist is not necessarily the best person on the team, just the purest. There's a fine line between pure code and good code. They're the equivalent of a staunch Conservative.

On the other end of the spectrum is the Hacker. Nothing can stop this person from finding a clever way around writing a bunch of code with a few well-placed exceptions to the given code. Sometimes, this is just what you need, but too much can be very bad for your code base. This person is most likely to write some assembly code in the middle of their C++ to make it faster and use constructs and edge cases in the language that most of the other programmers don't understand. Like the Purist, one of these on your team can be a real boon. It sometimes pulls the Purists back to reality and the hacker may offer a quick solution to a problem that a purist would take days or weeks to code. They're the equivalent of a staunch Liberal.

In the middle is the pragmatist or centrist. He believes in purity of code until the pure solution ends up being so complicated that a simple exception will easily do. He realizes that within every programming language or paradigm, there are some problems that just don't fit well. The Pragmatist is willing to think outside the box and consider alternatives.

For example, at Rocky International, we used a graphical programming language that was great for most of the work we had to do, but it didn't support looping over an array. We had a software component that needed to examine over two hundred Booleans and pack the results into an array for output. In any language, this would have been a quick looping operation. Unfortunately, the code needed to perform this task exploded into a huge module without looping functionality and yet we were supposed to write all of our code with this tool. We struggled along, but couldn't keep the application from crashing when we tested it. It was too big and the generated code was doing something screwy that we couldn't figure out. We were also nearing a deadline and needed this functionality. The developer working on this finally concluded that the best answer was to use the graphical tool for what it was good for, examining the incoming data, and use C for what it was good for, namely looping over the results and packing them together. The code shrank to 10% of its previous size and ran beautifully. It lacked the purity of the original, but nobody could argue that the final solution was elegant, too, especially because it finally worked.

Mr. Spock

Every now and then you'll run across a guy who reminds you of Mr. Spock, not to be confused with Dr. Spock, the pediatrician. For those of you who don't know, Mr. Spock was a character on the original Star Trek series, a science fiction program about the crew of the Starship Enterprise. Born on the planet Vulcan, Spock had a brilliant mind, was stronger than an average human, was seemingly tireless, and was extremely loyal to his captain. In one episode, the captain and Mr. Spock drink a serum that accelerates their metabolism so much so that they literally buzz around the ship, sounding like insects to the normal crew. At the end of the episode, Spock remains accelerated to "effect repairs around the ship."

At Ottobon, we hired Will, who had just gotten his PhD in engineering, not computer science. He had done some part-time work for us at BDI, so we knew he was a nice guy and figured we could train him in the mysteries of programming. Bob mentored him in how to structure object-oriented programs, check in code for builds, etc. It wasn't long, however, before Will started coming over to Bob's desk a couple of mornings a week with a printout of Bob's code showing where he had made a minor error by not checking a return value or something similar. This can be a bit humbling and some people might feel a bit insecure having someone like that on their team, but it's better to have a developer like that find your errors or ask why you're doing something that seems odd rather than having a bug report to fix later.

With more experience Will became more opinionated about the structure and inconsistencies of some of our code. He'd also get wind of changes that someone else might make to improve the structure of our code or that would require rippling changes to the rest of the code. It was not unusual to find that he had checked out over a hundred files to make changes overnight. If he was still working on the files in the morning and the files were still checked out, his mentor would send out a message stating that Mr. Spock was effecting repairs around the system. Having a Mr. Spock on your team can be very beneficial as long as he doesn't start stepping on other developer's toes by making stylistic changes for purity's sake.

Don't be afraid of having smart people on your team. As long as they're not a know-it-all, they can help make the rest of the team shine.

Wandercoding

Rich Hall is known for making up words and he published a couple of books on "sniglets" or words that aren't in our language, but should be. One of his words is *destinesia*, defined as "What happens when you enter a room but can't remember what you went for in the first place." I'm going to add my own word to the language of software development called *wandercoding*, defined as "What happens when you go to modify a chunk of code and it leads you to modify another chunk until you can hardly remember what you were trying to accomplish in the first place."

Almost everyone in software development has cat-like tendencies. It's so easy to get distracted while you're working on something. You need to add a call into your code from someone else's module. Then you notice that they're doing something horrible in their code or using some outdated calls that have since been deprecated. So, you decide to update that code. While you're at it, you notice that they've also got some inefficient data structures that might be the cause of some of the performance bottlenecks in the system. The next thing you know, you're doing a whole performance rundown on the system to see if there are other things you could be doing more efficiently. A week goes by and you finally get back to the job you had started. You've been wandercoding. You've improved the system's performance in some areas by 30%, but now you're behind on your project by a week. Your boss is pleased, but upset at the same time. See how easy it is to get distracted?

One former colleague, Adam, was a master of this. He generally did good work, but was so good at being distracted and wandering off course that he had a horrible reputation within the division because he was always behind schedule. He was always busy, but it was because he was working on something related to the internals of the system or on something that someone else needed for their work that was in his bailiwick. His code was often over-designed to handle every contingency, many of which would probably never be used.

He was also known for his remarkably bad judgment. At the beginning of one project, Adam and Bob were working on some functionality that they were interested in implementing. They reported that they were making good progress and their boss's boss wanted a demonstration of the functionality. The day before the demo, their manager, Frank, stopped by Bob's desk to see if they had a stable setup for the demo. He told Frank that they did and they were going to make sure that things went smoothly. The next day, Frank stopped by again and saw Bob fuming at his desk. They went somewhere to talk privately. He said that Adam had decided the evening before to merge in a bunch of his code. It was only going to take a few hours to do the job, but had actually turned out to be much more complicated than he originally thought. Bob was really angry because they wouldn't be able to give the demo now (they hadn't saved a runnable copy of the system) and felt that Adam was making him look bad in the process. It eventually took four days to finish the merge and get their project demonstrable. It was also fortunate that it was only an internal demonstration and wasn't for an important customer or a trade show as the timing would have been disastrous.

Frank's boss wasn't pleased with the general performance of the functionality and wanted to pursue it using a different approach. Adam and Bob were interested in doing the new work, but Frank's boss, having seen Adam illustrate his poor judgment once again, insisted that the project be given to someone else.

There's much to learn from Adam. First, he needed to be more closely monitored, not only for his tendency to wandercode, but also for his proclivity for making bad decisions. If you have a demo to give the next day, save a running copy of the application before you try merging new functionality. Adam would have been better off practicing a demonstration with the working copy to avoid using any unimplemented functionality anyway. Chances are your reputation at work will survive a minor screw-up or two unless you work for Dr. Evil. However, if the mere mention of your name conjures up images of failed prototypes, crashing demos, and consistently late software, your opportunities for future choice projects, significant pay raises, and possibly your employment will disappear as rapidly as a plate of freshly released _insert your most coveted techno-widget or anticipated software version here._

Discussion and Thought Questions

1. What kind of developer are you? What kind of developer do you want to be? What steps can you take to get there?

2. If you're a manager, what kind of developers do you have? Do you embrace their diversity or are you trying to make everyone the same? What strengths does your existing team have?

Chapter 12: The Rhythm Section –
Supporting Characters

Everyone you work with thinks their job is the most important and influential job in the company. They're wrong. Yours *is.*

- The author

Yes, the quote above is indeed somewhat a Zen *koan*. In some respects, everything is a matter of perspective.

You may notice or already have noticed that I seem to put the software engineers at the center of the software development universe. This is not entirely by accident. At the end of the day, you can have management, marketing, sales, and testing teams working for your company, but without the software development team, you won't have anything to sell. I've worked for companies with only software teams and little else and that's not great either. We had software, but it didn't sell very well.

I've already written about the sales, marketing, and management people you'll deal with. Now, I'll tell you about the other folks involved with a software company or project.

Watch Me Pull a Rabbit Out of My Hat

I'll start towards the beginning of the software development process. In larger or more mature companies (i.e. not small start-ups), the marketing folks will start the definition of a project, product, or product release. If your project is not commercial, then it's probably coming from some group that acts very much like marketing folks. Their job is to connect with the customer (whoever that may be for your project) and try to define an initial scope of work and timeframe for delivery. This is not usually an absolute – nobody can design and code the next generation whiz-bang operating system in a matter of months – so further negotiation is going to be required. One thing you can be sure of, it's most likely going to ask for more than you can dream of and in less time than you can fathom. As previously stated, it's usually a negotiation process. At Whistler, the number of features for the releases was getting so big and so much into the realm of "the software should just know that" that the developers started joking about it. They shot back that the next release of the software would start with a verbal description of the product that the end user wanted the system to automatically design. You would then pour in salt water and dirt and the computer would extract the required minerals, formulate the parts needed, and spit out your finished product. We'll get right on it! (Note: with today's 3D printers, only the first part of the joke is far-fetched anymore.)

Once an initial set of functionality is decided upon, someone has to decide what the product will look like. There may be some fancy user interface items such as toolbar buttons, dialogs, fancy controls, menus, etc. There's also going to be the desire to have some consistency to the entire system. Somebody has to take the general requirements for functionality and put it into a set of more specific items for the software developers to code. In some companies, the software developers may do this, but in many companies, there's another person or group responsible for this. At Ottobon, since we were writing commercial software, the product design team did this. They would generate design documents detailing the smallest functionality – what happens when this button is pushed, what the button looks like, how the menus look, what colors to use, etc.

At Rocky International, since this was a military application, this work was done by two sets of people. First, the systems analysts would produce a set of written and pictorial requirements to meet. Then there was a software requirements team that would take those specifications and turn them into more specific software requirements. Sometimes the wording was identical, but often, additional requirements were needed to cover cases that the initial requirements didn't touch.

If your company has a product design team or even just a product designer, it's a good idea to involve software developers in the design process. I've often seen product designers over-design features that the developers could have helped simplify from the start. Getting them involved early can save a great deal of time in software design, schedule estimation, feature design and redesign, and final feature negotiation. I've also seen product designers make incorrect assumptions about what functionality would be easier to implement that a developer could have easily corrected. Either way, I've seen a great deal of time and energy wasted, as well as features dropped that could have been easily retained, if only a developer had been involved early in the process.

I Think You Missed a Spot

A high quality product requires a high quality team to test your software. In my experience, the software developers themselves make horrible testers. If you add unit tests to your software, you'll certainly catch some things early and that's great. After that, you're best leaving the job to someone who likes to test code. It takes attention to detail and the desire to really try to find the problems in the software. Additionally, someone less familiar with the workings of the software will have no qualms about doing some of the most ridiculous things imaginable with it – just like your users will. As you might imagine, these people can be hard to find. In some companies, these folks are called software verification, quality assurance (QA), or testers.

Good people are invaluable to your product. At Ottobon, I had the pleasure of working with some very experienced QA people. They had worked at the company for years and had a lot of experience with many different products. As a result, they could set up test scenarios, especially for interoperating with the company's other products, much better and faster than I could. They found lots of bugs in our code – bad for us coders, but good for the customers. Good QA takes time and costs money. It needs to be planned well and needs to be complete. Anything they don't find will probably be found by a customer, so the more thorough they are the better. At times in my career, I thought that QA folks were simply a pain in the butt. Sometimes they really are, but most of the time, they're just folks trying to do their jobs the best they can. It's easy for them to bruise your ego when they come up with a whole bunch of problems with the software you worked so hard to produce.

QA involves both automated and manual testing of your code or system. Some of these folks may actually have significant coding experience themselves. Good or bad, they deserve your respect. Don't belittle them or consider them a nuisance, although some are. I have dealt with QA folks who create more work than they save. One guy would write up a ton of bugs that weren't bugs, simply because he didn't thoroughly read the specifications. I've always felt that as a QA person, you should start with the assumption that the software is working correctly, except in obvious situations where the application crashes. If something simply doesn't behave the way you think it should, check the requirements again to see if you missed something. Also, there's a big difference between a bug and something you just don't like. Software people hate getting bug reports that say things like, "When the software detected a problem with the incoming data, it showed a red warning message. Since it wasn't a real failure condition, it should be a yellow message. The specification says red, but I think it ought to be yellow."

I would get stuff like this all the time and it irritated the heck out of me. I might even agree with the bug report, but there's not much I can do with it. If the specification says red, I make it red. Send the bug report to the system designer team instead. If they change their spec, then I'll change my code.

When you add QA people to your staff, they're going to require training. I hate to say this, but that's really the QA staff's job. At Rocky International, we'd have a bunch of new people pulled into the QA team for every release. The developers were either busy with writing new code for the next release or fixing bugs on the current release. For the first release, we spent a significant amount of time getting the QA folks up to speed on how the software worked. We'd been writing the software for months and knew the requirements pretty well – there were a lot of them. After that release, more new QA folks came onto the team. Once again, they'd start writing bugs on the software that was working correctly. Why? Because the rest of the QA team didn't document or teach them how the system worked. So the developers would once again teach more folks how the system worked. I know it takes a village to educate a child, but I think that your parents should try to do it first and take some responsibility for it.

What's Up, Doc?

Documentation is one of my favorite things to hate. Good documentation can be invaluable and I'm always grateful when I need to refer to the documentation and it's actually useful. Documentation (or technical publications in some places) almost always gets the short end of the stick in any product cycle, however. For the most part, documentation writers are just that – writers. They usually get their technical background from the developers and what they figure out by using the software. Because they tend to come from a liberal arts background, they often think a little differently than the engineers from whom they need to dig information. They'll ask you about some functionality or try to guess from using the software and come to a perfectly logical explanation for the software's behavior – except that it's completely wrong.

I've written documentation before (more on that later), so I know that it's not an easy task at times to make some obscure concepts perfectly clear to some possibly non-technical users. The users want things in plain old English (or whatever their native tongue is). They don't want to wade through numerous references, allusions, and hyperlinks to get a simple answer to their simple question, but that's what they're usually given. So, when your documentation person asks you about a new feature in your software, be as helpful, patient, and verbose as you need to be to help them really understand what it's all about. A quick reply to get rid of them will only cause your customers to start calling your helpline and clogging up your message boards looking for the answers they should have been given in the first place.

Like good QA people, good documentation people are quite valuable and sometimes hard to come by. Imagine living someplace with a bunch of people who don't speak your language and don't seem to be able to give you the time of day when you need help. On top of that, they're trying to do a whole release cycle's worth of documentation at the end of the cycle, when the software is well defined, not changing constantly, and stable.

The best documentation people that I've worked with were completely anal about getting it done and done right. They knew that it would help users and really did make a difference to the perception and usability of your product.

I've also worked with some bad documentation people. I took one of these guys out to lunch shortly after he started working for us and started to tell him about our software. Everything was fascinating to him, but it was clear that this was probably his first technical product documentation of this kind. It was going to be a long journey for him and after a few months, it was clear that it just wasn't for him.

Welcome to DIY Documentation Warehouse

For a long time at Whistler, we didn't have any of our own documentation people. So, we wrote some of our own. For the highly technical documentation of the API (Application Programming Interface), this was fine. For the rest, it could have been better, but simply wasn't, mainly because nobody really wanted to do it. For the first release of our software, we hired an outside firm to do the documentation for us. We provided them with the basic material and it was their job to turn it into a manual. The thing was, they never came and talked to us. In addition, it became clear that they didn't even read or fix most of it. As Bob was the creator of the graphics and geometry code, he had written a description of the geometric primitives that you could use in building a 3D model. He was younger then and a bit on the free-spirited side. He included the following descriptions, which I quote verbatim from the manual, which I still have from 1987.

> Extrusion
>
> These are general 2d-profiles which are extruded into the third dimension (cosmic, eh?). They are specified by a vertex-list (a list of lists of 2d points, which may include commands such as circle, fillet (described elsewhere; translation – "you find-em.") or even interactively on the screen), and an extrusion distance.
>
> Revolution
>
> These are general 2d-profiles which are rotated about an axis into the third dimension (and you thought extrusions were hot shit). They are specified ...

I think you get the point. Bob took a lot of ribbing for that from his colleagues and a few customers, but he was incredulous that it had made it into the final publication of the manual. It was certainly not his intent that a customer should ever see that. Later that year, the manual won an award – not for the contents, but for the design. It was a very slick looking package, even if the contents weren't as useful as they should have been. As Billy Crystal playing Fernando Lamas used to say, "It's better to look good than to feel good and dahling, you look mahvelous."

Would You Like to Make a Deposit?

Having not learned our lesson after that, we hired a different company to write our documentation for the next release. They were very experienced...at writing documentation for ATMs (yes, automated teller machines.) All of the documentation for every menu item included a picture of the menu, the steps to get to the menu, and what that option would do. Doesn't sound so bad at first, does it? However, when some of these menus were nested, putting the same procedure and the pictures along the way in the manual for every option was unbelievably time and space consuming. This was great for ATMs, but not so great for software. It was usable, however, and proofread (thank goodness).

Different software calls for different kinds of documentation. If your software includes an API, then you should document it in a format that makes it easy for a user to learn. One thing that's very clear: examples of common uses of the API are both crucial to understanding it and invaluable resources to your users. API documentation will likely be different from the kind of documentation that's useful for the graphical user interface for the same product. One more thing – if you provide API documentation, a) it should actually work, and b) it should be possible for the user to cut and paste it into their code. Finally, if you find that the API examples are long and contain lots of repeated code, you should probably improve the API to perform some of the repetitive actions with one call.

I Could Tell You That, But Then I'd Have to Kill You

I have used documentation for many other products. The most recent and probably most frustrating was the documentation for a French-made product. It was the perfect example of how not to go about writing it. The product, which I will call Blade, was a graphical programming language that generated code for you. In the process of doing so, it would generate an intermediate language that was useful only for that product. Most users, however, only used and cared about the graphical pieces of the product and what kind of code they would generate. Unfortunately, much of the documentation referred to the intermediate language, which nobody but the Blade developers understood. Between that, the circular references, dead ends, and functionality that wasn't even mentioned in the documentation, it was generally considered a joke and only to be used as a last resort.

For example, we had been trying to figure out how to do some testing coverage analysis with one of its built-in modules and couldn't figure out how to merge two results together, even though this was vaguely mentioned in the manual. Bob sent out a message saying that since we couldn't figure it out, we would do a workaround. Another guy who didn't actually use the software that much responded that there did seem to be extensive documentation on the functionality and asked if we had read it all. Bob responded with this, "As you know, Blade is written in France. Unfortunately the documentation was written by a native Hungarian who speaks only broken French. The French is then translated by a native Chinese speaker into English. The documentation is so bad that it has been banned in parts of Europe and several Middle-Eastern extremist regimes have issued a *fatwa* on the original writer." Nobody ever again asked the developers if they had tried to figure out how to do something with Blade by reading the manuals. The assumption is that they tried and simply couldn't get anywhere. Their technical support wasn't much help either.

I wish that there was an easy answer to bad documentation. One thing that can help is to have several people actually read it. The developer should read sections that are relevant to their area of expertise. Then someone who doesn't know the product very well should read it to see if it makes sense.

Sometimes, the very wording of a sentence can make the difference between a quick answer and hours of frustration on the part of the user. If you think you don't have the time to read over the documentation for your section of the system and that the documentation person *must* have done a good job on it, think again.

The Professor and Mary Ann

Remember the old TV show "Gilligan's Island"? You may have seen it when it was on originally or maybe on TV Land reruns. The original theme song had the words, "…with Gilligan, the Skipper, too. The millionaire and his wife. The movie star and the rest." After the first or second season, they changed it to, "…The movie star, the Professor, and Mary Ann." I guess they felt slighted since there were only seven of them and they were the only two left off. In that spirit, I wanted to mention some more of the people who help get software out the door.

Part of every product development cycle is a build system. Building your software nightly is a great way to make sure that things aren't being constantly stuffed into the system that aren't compatible. You may have one of the developers do this job and that may work great for a while. This can become a job in and of itself so you may eventually need or want to hire a build person.

Once you're close to being done and want to have some users test your software, you may need a Beta manager. If you work for a large company, there may be a team of people who handle this job for you. They line up customers, help with the distribution (much easier to do now in the day of fast downloads), monitor message boards, and organize customer feedback for you.

Nowadays, most commercial software isn't sent out as a few files that you can simply shove into a directory and run easily. DLLs (Dynamic Link Libraries) may need to be registered, the operating system needs to be informed of removal and repair options, etc. All of this work requires installation expertise, and having someone figure this out in a few days is unlikely especially if there's a lot to install. Your company may have an installation team or you may want to hire someone, perhaps a contractor with experience in this, to handle it. Don't underestimate the time it will take to figure out this stuff. If you plan to have your software officially sanctioned by Microsoft and get logo certification, proper installation is a requirement and certification can take a while as well.

There are plenty more people at different companies that may also get involved with your product at one time or another. I apologize to them for forgetting to mention them. I know that they think their job is the most important and influential in the company.

Discussion and Thought Questions

1. How good is the documentation or help for your product, web site, or other software project? Do users complain about it? Can someone who doesn't have intimate understanding of the inner workings read it and get answers? How can you improve it? Might making it easier to understand improve user adoption of your software?

2. How many bugs in your system are being found by your users? Did you know about them before you shipped?

Chapter 13: Human Racehorses

What's all this talk about Soviet jewelry?

- Emily Litella on *Saturday Night Live* misunderstanding the discussion on Soviet Jewry.

In every company larger than 10 people or so, there's a Human Resources department. They are your best friend and your worst nightmare rolled into one. I've worked with some very good and very bad people in this department, but there is more to the field than just the department and the people who work in it.

The Unit

In every large company, there is a secret department that operates out of the basement of the headquarters. They spy on what's going on, affect policies, and assassinate leaders of South American Banana Republics. It's the Human Resources department, sometimes called personnel, and they don't really do the last thing. Or maybe they do…

The people in HR can really make a difference in your company, both positively and negatively. The good folks are able to concretely answer questions, guide you through tough times, and help you organize something you want or need to do with a team. The interesting thing about them is that they play different roles at different times and that can make it hard to tell what side they're on. As an employee, I've gotten good advice on my career and help with problems I was having. As a manager, I've gotten good advice on how to handle problem employees and how to deal with some sticky situations. On the other hand, they are also employees of the company and if you're having trouble with the company, they walk a fine line in helping you deal with it. You may be better off getting some outside advice. If your company has an employee assistance program (EAP), they often have counselors that can talk to you on the phone. I have found them to be fairly helpful when you need someone to listen and offer unbiased advice.

150

On the other hand, HR can be very helpful with advice on possible incentives for your team to work harder as a deadline approaches, tell you about company policies, help you hire people (see more below), and figure out how to delicately put some things in writing on a performance evaluation (assuming you're forced to do them).

Analyze This!

One of the most onerous tasks a manager needs to do is to write performance evaluations of their employees. Employees don't seem to like them much either. At one point in my career I had eleven people reporting to me and that meant writing eleven evaluations. As a manager, it is not recommended that you simply jot down a couple of nice words about each of your employees either. The HR department will tell you that your people deserve your most honest and constructive effort.

The variety of ways that I've done this and had this done to me run the gamut from simple to complex. The simplest reviews were those written by my manager and delivered in a meeting with him. My first few years at Ottobon were fairly simple. The evaluation was a form with some categories of work abilities with check boxes and room for comments. You were asked to rate things like "Capacity for work" and if you met, didn't meet, or exceeded expectations for that ability. My favorite category was "Wears two hats." A couple of weeks before reviews were due, a colleague would come into the office wearing a wool winter cap over his baseball cap (reviews were usually in February) so that he could get good grades in this category. When his boss asked him to do a self evaluation, he'd comment on how he had met the expectations.

Years later, we were doing 360-degree reviews, which meant that your manager, your peers, and any subordinates that you had reviewed you. I would always ask my employees to review themselves as they often know what they need to improve upon. One of my guys would hand me back a form that said simply, "Keep doing the things I do well. Improve on the things I don't do well." Helpful, don't you think?

You are Number 6. I am Number 2

Did I mention that I really hate employee evaluations? It's a painful process that takes too long and usually involves hurt feelings. I would deliver evaluations to some of my folks that had constructive criticism that would occasionally offend them. The bottom line was the "final score" for that person. At the end of each form was a place for their rating from one to five. A "one" meant that this person was going to be fired for incompetence. A "two" meant that this person was going to be put on a performance plan or possibly fired. A "three" meant that they met the requirements for their job. A "five" meant that they walked on water this past year and went above the call of duty. A "four" meant that you didn't quite walk on water, but still "rocked".

After many years of receiving ratings of four and five on their evaluations, the practice of giving high marks was put under scrutiny. Instead of the manager deciding the score, all of the managers in our division got in a room and compared our people to establish a uniform rating for them. In addition, rating a person as a five was also suggesting that this person should be considered for a promotion to a higher place on the technical ladder. Naturally, this started just as I became manager of the group.

I entered this yearly meeting with what I felt were fair evaluations for my folks, usually threes through fives. However, one of the other software managers always had his folks ranked much higher, only fours and fives. He could never be talked down and this made the process ridiculous. One year he rated his best developer a five. He was promoted to the next level, higher than almost anyone in the room. The next year, the same manager wanted to give the same developer a five in his new position! When probed, he really didn't know what was expected of someone in that position.

In the end, I had to go to my team and convince everyone who used to get a four or five that getting a three was just fine. It actually made sense, but didn't make anyone happy. If you want to know more about why evaluations stink, read "Incentive Pay Considered Harmful" in *Joel On Software*.

A Year Boiled Down

If you do just a little bit of reading about performance reviews, you'll find a mix of those who love them and those who hate them as performance management tools. Nowadays, the scale is tipped mostly towards the hate end. Even so, HR departments around the world continue with them, despite their often-negative effect on employee morale. So, what do you do with them?

First, as a manager, try to keep things positive. The one part about the review process that I liked was seeing what I had done for the year and seeing what my direct reports had done as well. It was a good time to talk about personal desires for the next year – maybe attend a conference, take a training class, or just work on something different. If you receive negative feedback about one of your direct reports, turn it into a set of positive suggestions. For example, let's say that you have a developer who seems to write buggier than average code and your other developers are pointing this out on their feedback for this person. You can a) work on firing this person, b) tell this person about the feedback and berate them, c) put them on a performance plan that may lead to firing them or keeping them, or d) work on an improvement plan and keep it positive. The first three will end up with a depressed, unproductive employee. If your goal is to eventually have them leave, go ahead with one of those options. However, if you want to see improvement, take the positive route. Tell them that you'd like to improve the entire team's bug production and have them research some tools or techniques that can be used to reduce bugs.

Stan, another manager working on his product, had a pet project that Bob was working on.

Later, when Bob received his review from Sam:

The net effect of this was that Bob had simply learned not to trust either of the managers and that he needed to start covering his butt. If someone puts, "Learn to cover your butt," on a performance review, would you think that would help?

If you're a manager, treat this process with care. Your employees don't mind hearing constructive advice, but hate hearing it once a year as a surprise. If you're an employee, when your boss gives you your review, they're probably doing their best to treat you nicely so thicken your skin a bit. If you're an HR representative, think of some other way to get feedback to your employees.

As Smart as Maxwell

One of the things that HR people have gotten much more interested in is measuring performance. With this came the advent of S.M.A.R.T. goals. S.M.A.R.T. is an acronym for specific, measurable, attainable, realistic, and timely. The idea is that if you put a goal on your performance review there should be a way to see if and how well you did it when you review the goal next year or next quarter. The further stipulation is that the goal shouldn't be something that's so easy that you could do it without any effort. The biggest problem with these is that they're very difficult to write properly so that they meet all of the criteria of a S.M.A.R.T. goal.

In software, most of your job is doing tasks that you haven't thought of very far in advance. You design and program what you need for the next release. Now if you say that you'll do what needs to be done to make the next release successful, you can't really measure that because it's not very specific. Saying you'll do something on your review and having your assignment changed is also a common occurrence.

When I asked for help once with writing these goals for my team, my HR representative sent me a list that he really liked from some other teams. I'll tell you that they were too vague, too easy, or not actually measurable. Does that help? I didn't think so. If you have to write these, just do your best. If your boss doesn't like what you come up with, ask him or her to give you a good example. If you can use it, great. If they can't help or give you a good example then you've just convinced them that you shouldn't waste any more time on the whole thing. What you'll do instead is come up with something vague or immeasurable and live with it.

I'll Throw In a Set of Ginsu Knives

Likely, but not necessarily, at your review you'll also get your raise for the year and maybe a bonus. While I was a manager, I got to spread out two pots of money every year. The direction from HR was that bonuses should go to your best people, not the average ones. My personal feeling was that my people would be upset if they didn't get some kind of bonus, especially if they knew it was bonus time. Therefore, I usually gave everyone something. That's not to say that my best people didn't get more than the others did, however. I felt that everyone was part of the team and therefore everyone should share in the rewards. After all, even the bench players get a Super Bowl ring if their team wins.

I would use my raise pool to balance out people's salaries and reward people for good work and use the bonus pool to provide additional reinforcement.

There is No I in Team

Many employees routinely think of teambuilding exercises as a nuisance. They get a lot of bad publicity on television shows that often portray them as a sadistic display of machismo on the part of the boss.

One such exercise that I attended was at a week-long leadership class and the exercises consisted mostly of problem solving skills. We did some trust building by having someone fall backwards off the top of a ladder into the arms of the rest of the team. Then we did some group activities like figuring out how to get across a "river" (it was a parking lot) using some boards and platforms. It was a lot of fun. The group had a good time working together and doing some good-spirited competition with the other teams.

When Bob became manager of a group at Ottobon, he decided that he wanted to do a teambuilding day. He had read about a high-ropes course at a nearby university and thought it might be a good activity for his new crew. He arranged the day and talked about the kinds of activities he thought would be appropriate for a bunch of programmers of various ages, sexes, and sizes. His team was rather skeptical about the whole thing, but he encouraged them to keep an open mind and just go to have fun. That's exactly what happened. Much of what they did was physical, but not extremely so. They solved some problems together, sent people flying up in the air in a harness, and walked across a log bridge thirty feet in the air. They got outside for a day, had a load of fun, and got to know each other better. Every one of the group, even the grumpiest, still has good memories of that day.

The HR department at Ottobon organized a teambuilding day for our product group. We got together to do a project where different groups have to draw a large picture together in separate parts to be put together at the end. There's a lot of communication that needs to be done and some people have to act as managers to organize the groups. I think that people generally have less fun doing this kind of activity, but they are okay.

Stormin' Norman

One of the things I learned at leadership school is that teams perform differently at different times. Bruce Tuckman classified the state of teams into four categories: forming, storming, norming, and performing. Teams go through this progression.

All new teams start out a bit rough and it takes a while before they really gel. This is perfectly normal, actually, and should be expected. The same team on a different project goes through the same progression as well. When you first get started people need to get their heads around the new project and figure out who's going to take on what job. This is the forming stage. Eventually, most teams learn the project and their roles and get to the performing stage. Some teams don't gel very well at all when there are abrasive personalities in the group. Work will still get done, but it's likely that things will need to be shaken up at a convenient time.

If you're managing a new group, give them some time to figure out how they each fit in. You can facilitate this by simply assigning different aspects of the project to different people, but have regular discussion meetings and see who wants to swap tasks according to their interest. Of course, there will be some jobs that nobody wants and everyone will try to get rid of them. Unfortunately, you'll just have to assign them to a person or two.

End Around

While the Human Resources department can be very helpful at some things, one thing that they're not always great at is hiring people. They can be helpful in this capacity, but they often miss things that you wouldn't if you were doing the hiring yourself.

For this reason, I have always preferred to scan through resumes myself. I could usually tell if the resume was worth looking at in more detail within a few seconds.

If you're looking for a job, of course, this also means that going through the HR department is your worst option. Sometimes it's all you have, but it should be avoided if possible. If you know someone at a company, ask them to get you the name of a hiring manager or to put your resume on the manager's desk with a note from your friend. Take a look at the book *What Color is Your Parachute* by Richard Bolles. It's a great reference for job hunting and has statistics on how people really get hired. HR is not the best way for you to go, if you can help it.

There is No U in Team

In your career you may either be fired or have to fire someone. I had to fire someone once and it was a painful, stressful thing to do. It was clear that this person wasn't able to do the job so it needed to be done, but it's just not that simple in a big company. First, this person needed to be made aware of the fact that there was a serious performance problem. This meant that he needed to be put on a performance plan. Only after failing to live up to the plan could we actually go ahead with firing him. The main requirement was that we had documented issues in writing.

There were accusations of religious bias (he was Muslim), there were tears, and there was pleading. Even though I knew it was the right thing to do, even for the employee, it was an awful thing to go through. If you have to fire someone, just be honest, but caring about it. Be straight, tell them what the problems are, and why you feel this is what needs to happen. Give them the most generous severance package you can or feel is warranted. If there has been illegal or malicious activity then I'd be much more harsh.

If you have the displeasure of being fired, you have my sympathy and empathy. Take some time to examine the stated reasons for it, whether you agree with them or not. Then, get back on the horse and get going again. In your next job, if you really are good, you'll be back on the top of the heap soon enough and regain your confidence.

Explaining a departure of this sort to potential employers can be a bit embarrassing. Put the best paint coating on it that you can and try to be diplomatic. You might say, "My manager and I had different expectations" or "A new supervisor felt that they didn't need someone with my skill set anymore." If probed you can elaborate, but try not to come off sounding accusatory. People will usually appreciate your honesty if you don't sound like a whiner.

Discussion and Thought Questions

1. Are you connected with former colleagues and other people who might help you look for your next job?

2. Are the goals on your performance review taken seriously and reviewed in detail? If so, have you taken steps to make progress on them?

What Did You Say Scotty?

In this section, I talk about some technical stuff like software processes and some of my "best practices" for software development.

Chapter 14: Trains, Planes, and Automobiles – Software Processes

I call it the art of fighting, without fighting.

- Bruce Lee in "Enter the Dragon"

Part of any production of software is the process that governs it. I've been involved with numerous projects using numerous processes and I'll tell you what works, what doesn't, and what to expect when using them.

The Process of No Process

At my first job with Whistler, we worked for a manager who didn't know software at all. We worked for a company that didn't produce software. We were trying to create software that we didn't understand well with the only goal of providing a level of functionality that could begin to match our competitors within about six months. While this gave us a goal, it lacked quite a bit in specificity, which was fine for a while. We proceeded to buckle down and get to work. Six months later, we had what we needed, but kept going, because the software was still quite immature. The internal customers were starting to look at what we had done and a few had started prototypes using our software. The software was buggy, ever-changing, and somewhat unstable as we hadn't taken much time to think about actually going through the process of releasing it as a "finished" product. Since we had no deadlines and no schedule, we just kept moving. After about a year of work we had an internal customer who wanted this nailed down. We talked about releasing something in May and that month came and went without much fanfare. In October, we were still talking about the May release. At the time, it was quite funny. At most of the places I have worked since then, nobody would be laughing.

I later came to realize that this was actually a coding process known as "Code Like Hell", amongst other names. The Code

Like Hell process is mainly about coding without planning or scheduling. There may be a deadline or functionality goal, but progress toward it isn't tracked well, if at all. If the finish line is a date, you're never sure what's going to be done by that time, but you might just decide to stop coding anyway. If there's a functionality finish line, you may get there eventually, but have no idea when. When I was a young coder, I loved this process. It was mostly stress-free because the expectations were so vague. When you're just getting started with a project, this is a fine way to go, too. You might simply consider it a prototyping phase. Be careful not to let it go on too long, however. Eventually, you need to have a clearer picture of the timeframe, functionality, and quality you want.

For most companies, however, this approach is not going to fly anymore. There are other processes that have some of the freedom that this process allows without all of the uncertainty. Beware a company or group that seems like they constantly operate this way. It may be a lot of fun, but can be very dangerous. I saw BDI go from being worth millions to nearly nothing because of this mentality and it was anything but stress-free.

Buttermilk Falls

Have you ever noticed that almost any waterfall that doesn't have a big drop and isn't named after someone is called Buttermilk Falls? I have. If you discover some heretofore-unknown waterfall that trickles downhill rather than drops, think of another name. What does this have to do with processes? Nothing, sorry.

Well, sort of. There is a process called the waterfall method. This is one of the most commonly used processes because it's fairly straightforward to implement. First, you decide what you'd like to have in your software release. Then you do some estimating of the time to produce that software. You might do some design work, prototyping, or simply guessing at the time. Then you decide what's going to fit within the schedule for software development. At this point, you can decide to extend the schedule to fit the time needed to code, or drop some of the features to fit the coding time. Then you start coding, fix bugs, and release the software.

The whole thing is sequential and can involve tons of detail work to go into the scheduling of each coding task or simply end with an estimate of the entire task or feature. This process can work great if you're mainly interested in trying to keep some kind of handle on a release beyond what's provided by Code Like Hell. It requires a little flexibility later on because if things don't go according to plan something may have to change. You may need to drop a feature that doesn't fit, or decide to extend the schedule if that's an option. If you can be somewhat flexible and are working with flexible people, this process works just fine. I've used this many times and find it nice due to its simplicity.

The Irrational Unified Process

You may have heard of the Unified Modeling Language or UML. It was created by three guys who had each independently starting making their own modeling for object-oriented programming. They joined forces, started a company called Rational, were bought by IBM, and still produce very useful products and ideas. One of the things that Rational came out with was a process called the Rational Unified Process (RUP).

This is a form of waterfall method that has some names associated with each phase of the process. Inception is the planning stage. Elaboration is the prototyping and estimating phase. Construction is when the actual building of the software takes place in full. Transition is when the software is beta tested and delivered. You can look into this process on your own, as there's much more to it. I'll admit right here that I have never used this process as advertised.

When I worked for Ottobon, we used the Waterfall method with the RUP names. I dubbed it the Irrational Unified Process. The reason for this is that the flexibility of the Waterfall method in being able to drop a feature or modify the schedule was also eliminated. We would be given the feature set a month or two later than scheduled and start the elaboration process. This process would then vary widely in the time allowed. We would then estimate our software development time. These estimates were refined by the software team. Then the estimates would be met with sheer disbelief by the product-design and marketing teams. Quality assurance would estimate even more time to test the features than we took to develop them. After the battle of the feature dropping and modifying, we'd begin implementing. Any previously poorly defined features would take on a life of their own and expand. We would start to run behind schedule, but be expected to work overtime to catch up. We'd start working nights and weekends to catch up to the schedule. We'd hit our code complete date, but exclude a feature or two. Quality assurance would assure us that they couldn't test the software as it was too unstable and tell us that we really weren't code complete. We'd fix bugs like crazy working nights and weekends. We'd release the software, but nobody felt like celebrating.

Anything here sound rational to you? If only we could have used the process as originally intended, maybe it would have. I'm sure that it was put together better than the process we used. Here's the real lesson: if you take a process and its jargon, try to use it as closely as possible to its original form. Then you'll know if it's really worth anything.

Man Overboard!

After a few releases using the irrational process described above, the group Vice President made a directive that we begin to put the Capability Maturity Model Integration (or CMMI) into place. I watched some of our managers go to training at the Software Engineering Institute (or SEI) of Carnegie Mellon University. CMMI is a process that's very detailed in what you should be doing without telling you how to go about doing it. The implementation is up to you. For example, I've seen articles written on using the Rational Unified Process to implement CMMI. The whole point of the CMMI process is to get your organization operating at a higher level and to ascertain your current level of operation. The levels are detailed by the SEI and go from 1 to 5. A level 1 organization is one that may or may not be able to produce or reproduce software development performance from one project or release to the next. A level 2 organization is called a Managed one. They can produce software with the expectation of repeating performance on the next release. This gradually works up to a level 5, or Optimizing, which only a few companies ever achieve, but which says you really rock at producing high-quality software on schedule.

Most upper level management people in the software industry have heard of this and so have many software customers. Of course, customers like the sound of having their software produced by a company with the equivalent of the Good Housekeeping Seal on it, so they've started asking their software suppliers what level they are. Upper management thinks this is a great way to spur on their organizations to greater efficiency and direct their software teams to start implementing a plan to get to the next level.

There's only one problem with this. This process works great for some kinds of software and is complete overkill on others. If you have software that needs to operate in life-or-death situations, then you should strongly consider this. Are you writing a game, coding for a web site, or writing software that doesn't have to be military grade? Then this is probably not what you need. I'm sure that there are pieces of the process that might help you improve your management of the release cycle and you should definitely look into them, but going whole hog is likely to send your productivity into a tailspin.

I used this process at Rocky International after I saw Ottobon starting to implement it. Rocky was using it for flying helicopters so it seemed like a reasonable thing to do. Every step of the software development process was well defined, from design documents to requirements tracking. There was a database of requirements and links from each requirement to the function in the code that implemented that requirement and vice versa. Can you imagine trying to do that on most products? Well, it's a CMMI requirement, but on most products does anyone care what functions or classes actually implement the features? In fact, most of the products that I worked on didn't have individual requirements laid out in a fashion that would allow for this kind of cross-linking. For Rocky International, it was imperative to have a process like this built in.

The funny thing is, even with all of the built-in process at Rocky, the software is still filled with bugs. It's impossible to simply eliminate them by edict, not that CMMI actually tries to do that. In the end, the process still involved a lot of testing, fixing, and retesting of software.

Agility Tests

In the past several years, there has been a backlash in the software field against the rigid and unrealistic demands of people outside of software. Unfortunately, the state of the art in software development is that writing software isn't like building a house. Software's innate flexibility and malleability make it different from more solids-based construction. And so the new buzzword is Agile software development. The main goal of Agile software development is to try to get back to reasonable planning and scheduling, flexibility in features or deadlines, and yet producing usable software.

Some of the agile processes use a very small, very tight waterfall method, but over the period of three or four week cycles. These cycles continue until the given deadline arrives or the feature set is complete. By operating in short-term timeframes, this process keeps every aspect necessarily short and to the point.

There's a Small Multi-Legged Creature Crawling on your Shoulder.

Mr. Spock said this to a security guard to distract him in the original Star Trek series. These same multi-legged creatures distract us from our software goals in the form of "Feature Creep." You may know this by another name, but the basic idea is that as a release is being developed, the marketing and sales people are still talking to customers and the product designers are still being creative. The net result is that they will try to cram more features into the software release that you're trying to build and this can be bad. As you probably already have more than you can handle built into the schedule, this new or enhanced functionality is not going to appear magically in the finished product without having an impact on the schedule. That's the first thing you should point out if this happens to you.

You can be polite about it, but you should be firm. Tell them (whoever is trying to get the feature added) that adding this feature is going to take you X amount of time. Suggest that it should either be dropped, saved until a later release, or another feature that's yet to be coded be dropped instead. Unless you can really just add this without any real impact (don't forget your design, estimation, and debugging time), you've got to be honest with the powers that be or you'll be the one with your feet held to the fire when you're late. Also, be sure that the Quality Assurance and Documentation teams are notified and can add their estimates. Enlightened management already knows that there's an impact and will ask you what the impact is. They'll also be working on what the appropriate response should be. Unenlightened management will not have a clue how to handle this properly. Straighten them out immediately.

I should point out that some processes that are more iterative in nature allow for feature creep by simply changing the features to be included in a future iteration. If feature creep is a big problem where you work, look into a process that embraces it, build some extra padding into your schedule, or have a plan for dealing with it. I have yet to work on a product or project that didn't have feature creep, so ignoring it is not a good option.

Discussion and Thought Questions

1. What process do you use or have you used? Does it have some of the flaws pointed out in these descriptions? How can they be overcome?

2. Do you have another process that you can recommend to your company that might work better than what you're currently using?

Chapter 15: It Doesn't Get Any Better Than This – Best Practices

I can tell you that this release will not go smoothly. 1.0 releases are the worst things to design and predict. Don't say I didn't warn you.

- The author

There's not enough space or time to include all of the best practices of software development here in this book. I can just point you to other books specifically about that, such as *Rapid Development* by Steve McConnell. What I will do here is outline a few things that are important and will help you in your development work to make life easier and more efficient.

Maybe Something in Plaid

Design work is vital to your coding and development work. I've had too much work become much more difficult due to bad design work on my part or others to give short shrift to the design at the beginning. The amount of design work to perform should be proportional to the amount of work you're talking about. At one company, things were going a bit overboard on the design side. At one point we joked that in a few years we would spend our 10 month development cycle doing 8 months of design work to decide which single line of code to change. We would change that line of code in an hour and then test it and document it for the next two months.

Of course, this is a bit of an exaggeration, but there's a time to design and a time to code. Spending them efficiently and wisely is a delicate balancing operation. I've spent an hour designing small changes and weeks designing large systems. The amount of code and the impact to the system are important in deciding how much time to spend in design.

One thing I recommend is that, if possible, you include a prototype in your design work. Nothing is more frustrating than doing a design simply by reading some code that you'll be enhancing and writing a design document on the changes you'll make. Then, when you go to implement it, you find out in the first twenty minutes that you picked the wrong code to modify. You would have figured this out quite easily if you had actually tried to add the code in the first place. Then, you'd have found all of the other classes that are affected by this change when you couldn't compile it. If you decide to do a prototype, step back periodically and take a critical look at what you're producing. Do your interfaces look clean? Are the classes designed logically? Have you already started writing spaghetti code and you've only been working on it for a day? Prototypes need not be long exercises. Even getting started on writing the code can get you involved in learning what useful pieces of code already exist, what needs to be modified, and how to best add the new functionality.

Even though you've started with a design for your code, let's add this – never stop designing your code. Even as you near the end of your coding, you should think about whether your design was optimal. You may not want to change it at any particular moment, especially due to time constraints, but maybe you can document your suggested improvements for implementation at another time.

Upon Further Review, the Ruling on the Field Stands

Design reviews are often treated as a nuisance. I know that I always felt this way about them, but this is probably because I'd never experienced too many helpful ones. It always seemed like they were just going to slow me down.

I've since learned that these can have great value if done well. At Rocky International, there were two design reviews for every project – a high level and low level. On the down side, most of the things brought up in these design review meetings related to the documents rather than the work. Since everything had to conform to a certain document format this was necessary, but it gets a little tiring hearing about your table of contents being out of sync with the actual pages of the document or that the version of another document you were referencing had changed.

Mostly what I did when I reviewed someone else's document was look at the design of the actual code. I could read the requirements and see if I thought that the design was set up to handle them properly. This often brought up issues that were missed by the developer or taught me something that I didn't know yet.

I'm not big on writing huge documents about designs that usually go unread or are out of date as soon as they're written, but it makes sense to have at least critical portions of the system or feature reviewed by others. They might find potential performance or design flaws earlier in the development cycle this way. It's also a chance to have the developer educate the rest of the team on how something new will be implemented or something old will be modified.

Please Wait a Moment While I Process Your Request

Pick a process that meets your needs. There are numerous development processes and cycles that are used in software development. Some of them are stifling and some are so free-form that they hardly exist. I've never been big on highly defined and regimented processes, but I'm not anti-process either. I've just seen some people try to force a development cycle to go perfectly smoothly by inflicting a rigorous process on it as if that's all it would take. "If only we design it like crazy so that we know everything up front and won't have any questions about anything later, we'll be able to do great project estimates and produce on time," they'd say. Then, when things don't go as well as hoped, they would say, "We just have to work harder at it and get better at it. We'll do even more design work this time!"

Theoretically, if you spent so much time designing everything almost down to the lines of code you needed, then you'd probably be right. You'd probably overshoot your ship date by

100%, but you'd know everything and be done exactly when you said you'd be done. You still wouldn't have gotten done any faster, just more reliably.

Nowadays, some lighter processes are being adopted. They include shorter milestones, incremental design work, and periodic "releases." On the down side, you have to fight the marketing and executive folks who often want to know everything up front. On the plus side, you might convince them that you can be more flexible with functionality and release dates if you go this route.

Whatever you decide on, I recommend periodic internal releases. Every once in a while during your release cycle, get the software into some kind of shape. Build it and test it for a week or so. Fix some of the major bugs and some of the minor ones, too. You'll have something that can be demonstrated at trade shows or shown to customers for a while as you continue developing the rest of the software for that release.

Picking almost any process at all is usually better than not having any process. Even a simple implementation of the Waterfall method (define, design, code, and test) with some milestones will give you something to shoot for and have an idea of where you are and where you're headed.

Jeepers

You must fight feature creep. Halfway through your development cycle someone will come along and try to cram more stuff into your carefully planned release. Don't just roll over without a fight. Exchange something old for something new. Do some analysis on the new feature. Often these things turn out to be poorly considered whims that don't fit into the theme for the whole release or go counter to the way that the rest of the system works. Chances are it hasn't been given the same considered system design work that the rest of the features have. Make sure that it does before you implement it and make sure that the impact of implementing it is known and accepted.

Warning: Construction Will Be Done Nightly

Once you have something worth building, do it automatically every day. Nighttime is often a good time to do this as everyone in your group will have the whole day to make sure that they get their files in shape for the build.

If the build doesn't compile or link then you only have one day's changes to wade through to figure out what went wrong. Usually build problems aren't too hard to track down and I'd guess that more than half the time we had them it was just that someone had forgotten to check in a file that they had changed or a new one that they had created into the source control system.

Check This Out

Once you're past the initial prototype stage of the first release of a product, you should be using a source code control system (SCCS). Note: This is often referred to as software configuration management nowadays. There are freeware and commercial versions available. Try out a few and decide what you think gives you the features you need. Some of them have different work paradigms so make sure that you can understand (and don't hate) the way that source control system operates. For many years I worked with a system that was universally vilified by most professionals. Although it had problems, and some of them were indeed horrible, at least it was straightforward and let you do what you needed to do.

Make sure that periodically, while you're developing, you can reproduce a working version of your system so that it can be debugged for demonstration purposes. Just when you think this isn't important, because the Marketing group told you that you weren't going to that big conference, you'll be heading there in a week.

One final requirement for the SCCS – it should have scripting capabilities. That is, you should be able to add code to your nightly build scripts that get code out of your SCCS without human intervention. I've seen too many builds break because

175

the buildmeister made a mental error in getting files. Also, if the buildmeister isn't around and someone else needs to run the builds, training is far simpler. The goal should be to automate all of these repetitive processes.

Smoke on the Water

Now that you're doing nightly builds and using a good source control system, you'll want to make sure that the previous day's changes aren't messing everything up. So, first thing in the morning it should be someone's job to get the latest build and run a "smoke test". This is usually a short series of basic tests on crucial system elements, e.g. file save and load (a.k.a. persistence), printing, installation, and other tests unique to your product. If you do this, you'll know that nobody checked in any code that significantly degraded the quality of the system. If you don't pass the smoke test, then you only have one day's changes to wade through to figure out what happened. Problems that cause the smoke test to fail can be more difficult to trace, but at least you'll have a limited set of changes to examine.

Later in your release cycle, when you're in the final bug fixing stage, it's often beneficial to have a regression test (a more complete smoke test) performed for each fix. This doesn't have to be a horrible task, but should include some common functionality that tends to break frequently. After each bug fix, run through the regression test to make sure that your code changes don't break the tests.

Dominance and Submission

One of the things a couple of companies did was to use submission documents. When you checked in your code, you filled in a simple form with information about what the code was for, what files and versions were involved, and what bugs you (may have) fixed. This document was checked into the source control system and emailed to your colleagues. Although writing these was somewhat tedious, they were very helpful in seeing what files went together as a bug fix or new code submission. If the build broke or a new bug crept into the system, you might be able to spot what happened by reading through some of these documents. They were also very helpful in tracking who was doing what. Several people would read these after returning from vacation to see what had been going on while they were away. Another benefit was that simply reviewing your submission documents for the week made it easy to write your weekly status report.

These documents were referenced in the bug tracking database and the comments for the files that were checked in. This allowed for easy cross-referencing. If you knew the bug, the file(s), or the submission document, you could trace any desired information from there.

Put Down the Keyboard and Step Away From the Code!

As your release date gets closer, you'll likely be pushing to fix all of the bugs in the system. If you're not using a bug tracking system – and you should be – then you'll probably be using a common spreadsheet or some other method. All of the bugs in your system should be rated according to their severity and desirability to be fixed before release.

It's unfortunate, but your software is probably going to ship with some known bugs in it, simply because it needs to get out the door on time. However, just because you have a bug doesn't mean it should be fixed. First of all, bug fixing time shouldn't just be a free-for-all. Developers are more likely to spend time fixing the "low-hanging fruit." These are the easy bugs to fix or the ones in the developer's own code that they find most embarrassing. You may wish to let them have some time to do that, but then you should really concentrate on the most important bugs – the ones that crash the system and block functionality from working. Towards the very end of the release, only specific bugs should even be permitted to have fixes. This will prevent the "fix one bug, create two more" syndrome from keeping your release from shipping.

Managing this time well gives you the opportunity to truly control the quality of the software you send out and when it gets sent.

Zamboni™ Time

What time is it? A Zamboni is a machine that cleans the ice in a rink. At a hockey game, the Zamboni comes out between periods to make the ice smoother and faster. It gives a fresh start to each period.

In the same vein, giving your developers a couple of weeks (or more if you have the time) to clean up is a great way to ease into the next release cycle. Let them fix some of the bugs you didn't have time for in the previous release or clean up some code that was sub-optimally designed or written. When I was a manager, my folks asked me for some time to do this at the beginning of one release. Since we had some time before the new features were designed, it was approved. They made great use of the time and felt that they had "clean ice" to start the next release on.

Sorry, But We're Out of Coors Light®

It's been said by many, but started by Fred Brooks in *The Mythical Man-Month*, in software development there is no silver bullet. In developing software, there's no magic solution that makes all of your worries and problems disappear. Find a set of tools that fits your needs best, then get to work. Pick a programming language that's suited to the work and has functionality that's helpful. You wouldn't code a web site in C and you wouldn't write a spreadsheet application in Perl (well at least I wouldn't). There are plenty of technologies available in many areas of software, so there's no reason to reinvent the wheel. If you can find a package that will help you, then by all means use it. Be forewarned! I have rarely used a third party package that didn't require some customization or have some issue(s) that had to be worked around. In the end, however, you eventually have to get to work with the best tools you have available.

The next few suggestions fall into the category of "Personal Best Practices.

Welcome Back to DIY Warehouse

On one of Bob's projects, he managed a developer who was programming an API (application programmer interface) that read and wrote files in a particular format. The API was for customers who wanted to work with those files. Bob took a look at the API and couldn't understand a bit of it. He felt like the API needed an API to make it simpler to use. As one colleague put it, "The API shouldn't be so difficult to use that it's easier to just do the work yourself."

I've worked with code in the past that was so well designed that simply looking at the class definition or getting auto-help in the development environment was all you needed to know how to use it. I've also worked with code that was so convoluted that I had to start reading it to see if it was even the correct code for me to call.

Every code that you write should be written like it's an API for someone else to use. In the end, it will make your code more likely to be reused and you'll be able to understand it later when you need to modify or use it. If you take this philosophy, people will begin to compliment you on your code when they use it. For a programmer, there's no better praise.

No Ad-libbing, Just Stick to the Script

Every developer who has given their share of software demonstrations knows that there's nothing worse than running into "the demo factor". You've prepared your scenario, gone over the functionality you want to show, and you're ready to go. Suddenly in the middle of the demo, gremlins have somehow crept into the code or the machine and are wreaking havoc on it. The functionality doesn't work or the application crashes and you feel like an idiot. I don't know why this happens, but it does.

I was preparing to give a demo to another team within my company. I knew that some parts of the software were unstable, but had worked out a basic script to follow that would allow me to sidestep the landmines. Just before the demo, one of my colleagues told me that a particular path in the UI was more stable than the others. I don't know why I listened – perhaps it was the power of suggestion. My mind wrapped around his suggestion and I changed what I had rehearsed. You guessed it, the system crashed repeatedly and I blew my opportunity to impress the other team. Why didn't I just follow the script that I knew worked?

Unfortunately people always seem to remember the worst stuff that you show them. This is one of the reasons that teachers generally do not show the wrong way to do something – students always remember the wrong way, too.

When you have a demonstration to give, practice it. Then stick to the script. You can add some extra ad-libbing at the end if people ask for it. It's better to leave them wanting more than to leave them with the impression that the system is held together with frayed string.

The Buck Stops There

You've just added some new code to the user interface and you're testing the system. You go through a series of steps and BOOM, the system crashes. Your first thought, of course, is that you've just found a new bug in the system. What has really happened, however, is that you've just created that bug.

It's a common problem in working with a group of developers to think that the problem you've just found isn't the result of what you've just done. The code you just added is simply too far removed from the problem. The answer is simple – when you see a problem, assume it's your fault. See if you can disable your new code (all of it) and see if the problem still manifests itself. If not, you've done something to make it happen. It may well turn out to be a coding error on someone else's part, but that doesn't absolve you from trying to fix it anyway or at least informing the other person. The buck stops with you.

S.E.P. Fields

In Douglas Adams' classic science fiction series *The Hitchhiker's Guide To The Galaxy* he describes the S.E.P. field. It stands for "somebody else's problem." The interesting thing about an S.E.P. field is that you can't see it if you're looking straight at it; you can only see it out of the corner of your eye. This is because it's not your problem, it's somebody else's. My personal feeling on this is that on a team, if you see a problem, at least point it out. It may be something that you really can't solve, but the person who can may not even know about it. Politely point it out to that person and/or the project manager, who may want to track it and make sure it eventually gets solved.

Odo the Shape-Shifter

When you're at work, you're working and you need to have a work persona. Sure you may be a wild person outside of work, but at work, you're as professional as you can be. Yes, you can still have a personality, but there are some things to avoid.

Don't send flame emails. If you get angry about something, go talk to the person or vent to a colleague. Flame emails are universally hated and can become a permanent record of your behavior. In an effort to curtail his flammable nature, one colleague would routinely write an email and send it to himself. Later in the day, he'd decide if he should send it to everyone else or if he had simply needed to vent and had already gotten it out of his system.

Your online persona outside of work can get you in trouble at work. It is my sincere hope that you work for a company that doesn't try to invade your personal space by searching the internet for your blogs, Facebook entry, MySpace entry, or any other websites looking for dirt on you. However, enough people have lost their jobs or not gotten job offers due to the prevalence of information that you can find about people. Keep your profile low and on the straight and narrow and you won't have any problems.

Farnsworth! Take a Memo

One of the things I learned in college as an engineer was to keep a lab notebook. There were a number of rules to follow, as this was a potential legal document. Although I never worried about the legal aspects as a software engineer, the one thing I did was write everything in a notebook. I preferred an 8 x 10½ notebook with quad ruling (graph paper), because it helped me draw diagrams, but the choice is yours.

I wrote down *everything*. If I was designing a set of classes, I'd jot down the ideas in the notebook. If I had a list of tasks to perform, they went in there, too. For tasks, I would put a hollow square on the left side of the page. When it was completed, a check mark went in the box. This way I could always go back a few pages and see what still hadn't been done.

At the end of the year, when it came time to write my performance review input, I was able to scan through my notebook and see what I had done for the past year. Keeping all of this information in one place made the notebook kind of messy, but I always knew where to find it. I highly recommend it.

Discussion and Thought Questions

1. What are you doing that you consider a best practice? What aren't you doing that you should be?

2. Do you have anything that you do personally that you consider a personal best practice? Share this with your manager. Perhaps he or she can spread this to other developers and improve the whole team.

In the End

No, this is not where you should "take it." All of the preceding sections have been about the people and things that you should know and do that will affect your career. This section is about what to do with that information.

Chapter 16: Of Forks and Knives - Your Career in Software

Walk left side road, okay. Walk right side road, okay. Walk middle, squash like grape.

    - Mr. Miyagi in his advice to the kid in "Karate Kid."

That way's nice. But, that way's nice, too.

    - The Scarecrow in "Wizard of Oz."

Your career is a lot like cutlery. Forrest Gump said that life was like a box of chocolates and that may be so, but careers are like cutlery. You'll be faced with forks occasionally and need to decide which tine to follow. Knives may come along that sever, or threaten to sever, your connections and your grounding. Spoons are used to collect things along the way, be they accolades, money, satisfaction, knowledge, or friends. Don't you hate it when people make lame analogies like that? I know I do.

Jack of all Trades or Master of One

We've talked about the personalities of the engineers on a team so now we'll talk about what kind of engineering focus you want. Engineers fall into two main categories, namely generalists and specialists. A generalist is the equivalent of a liberal arts major in college. They get a broad educational background without much focus on a particular subject, but they have learned how to think, how to learn, and how to communicate. Put them on a task, give them some guidance and they'll get going. A specialist is more like the military history major. Sure, it's part of a liberal arts education, but this person is much more interested and adept at this particular topic. Give them something else to research and it will get done, but with less enthusiasm and less brilliance than something that's right up their alley.

In software, a generalist might still have a specific area that he can generalize within. For example, I have spent most of my career in computer aided design applications. I have some specialized knowledge in graphics and geometric modeling, but I still consider myself a generalist as well due to my experience in designing many parts of whole applications. However, I have no experience at all with web applications and web sites. So, this makes me a generalist in desktop applications, with some areas of specialization.

A true specialist is more like my colleague, Arlo, who was fantastic at what he did. No matter how many software releases we went through, there was almost always more work related to his specialty to perform. However, given a different project that was out of his realm, he'd move much more slowly and be much more insecure about completing it.

In your career, you may be given the opportunity to specialize in some aspect of your work. If you choose to do so, specialize in the field, not the technology. For example, you might be very interested in computer graphics. If you wish to specialize, however, in the long run, it's better to be an expert in computer graphics than an expert solely in Microsoft DirectX. Not to say that you may also be extremely knowledgeable in that technology, but what if you decide to go to work for Apple? A graphics person who understands the fundamentals and commonality of different graphics technologies will be much more marketable than just a DirectX expert. Do what you can to keep fresh in the latest developments and newest technologies of your specialty or you may find yourself a dinosaur who's stuck doing maintenance on outdated code.

Follow the Yellow Brick Road to Perdition

No, you don't have to skip or sing. This is a journey up the technical ladder of your company or companies throughout your career.

A former manager used this analogy to illustrate roles in software development based on Kool-Aid®. "Bill," he said, "when you're a junior engineer, you are expected to show up at work, do your best, and try not to screw up. You drink the Kool-Aid. When you get to senior engineer, you have more responsibility and you serve the Kool-Aid. A principal software engineer at the highest level is expected to mix the Kool-Aid." Now when I tell people the Kool-Aid story, they mostly don't get it. At the time I did, perhaps because I had heard it from him before and had more context to it. His basic point is that the higher you get on the software development leadership ladder, the more you're expected to buy into and promote the philosophy and strategy that your management lays out for you. Even if you disagree with them in private, you should support it in public. I still have a hard time with this occasionally, but politics is important in your career and the sooner you accept it, the better off you'll be in the end.

There really is a ladder for software engineers to climb if you want to climb it. Some companies do a better job than others in telling their engineers about it and some managers do, too. Also, some companies do a better job at helping their engineers climb the ladder than others.

Unfortunately, most companies (even some large ones) do a poor job of this. Part of this is a lack of management training on the subject; part is because the way work is done there doesn't support a clear roll for different levels of engineers. In many companies, everyone's simply a software engineer. Senior engineers will be recognized with higher salaries and bonuses, but may not have any other clear demarcation. Some engineers exhibit more leadership, while others are technically more adept.

At one former company, there were several levels, but their meaning was not well understood by either the managers or the developers and I brought this up to my HR representative one day. He admitted that it wasn't well publicized. Additionally, in all of the day to day activities, most managers don't have time to worry about the details of promotions and responsibilities for their engineers. Finally, many engineers don't really care about their career paths that much. Some certainly do, but most of the ones I've worked with simply wanted challenging work, good pay, and reasonable expectations. They were happy if they were given a promotion (most of the time), a raise, a bonus, or stock options, but didn't spend a lot of time thinking about how to make it better next year.

At one company, things actually worked backwards. Nobody in the group wanted to be promoted above a certain level. The expectations were too high and the details of those expectations were too vague. Oh, HR had a listing of them, but most engineers had never been judged by them. The feeling in the office was that being promoted was kind of like being the current mole in "Whac-A-Mole." When your head was above the board, you were likely to be pounded or have your head severed from the rest of your body. Is it any wonder that nobody else wanted to be promoted?

Promotions at this company were also done by committee. The manager of the employee in question would recommend an engineer and a group of managers would add their own experiences with this person. One of my fellow managers spoke the praises of one of his employees and recommended promotion to the next level, which was at the level of Corporate Fellow. Nobody questioned that this person was extraordinary and the promotion passed. The next year, however, when we reviewed the same person, his manager said he was doing an amazing job even considering his new level of responsibility. When probed, however, his manager didn't really know what was expected of a person at that level. How can you judge someone relative to a standard if you don't know what the standard is?

As you climb the corporate ladder, you'll have the opportunity to do so by going through the management chain or the technical chain. The management chain is much better defined as you know in most companies who your boss is and who their boss is. The technical side is trickier to tell and sometimes is more about what you contribute, can contribute, and are expected to contribute. Whether you take on a higher level of technical leadership by having it thrust upon you or whether you seek it out, it's best to establish the expectations at the beginning. Ask for a written list of responsibilities and how you'll be judged on them. Ask how you'll improve things that you're not good at that may be on the list. Will you get training, be mentored, or simply be given a pass on some of those responsibilities?

Donkey Kong and Lemmings

In your career, you can decide that you want to take control or go with the flow. Most of the software engineers I know have been of the latter type. No matter what you choose, and not making a choice is a kind of choice as well, you should be open to opportunity. A friend was offered the opportunity to teach a class at a local university. Although he wasn't confident that he could do it, with the urging of colleagues and his family he accepted. He really enjoyed the experience and was commended by the students on his teaching ability. Some of the things he learned while teaching the class were then put to use on our product.

Even within the boundaries of comfort in a particular job, you may have opportunities to branch into different areas of software development. For example, you may be a database expert, but have the chance to work on user interface code for a while. Take the opportunity to broaden your knowledge base and experience.

While you're working, take the time to see beyond your local area of responsibility and get a feel for the how the whole system fits together. It will help you diagnose problems, improve your designs, and open doors to new possibilities in your career. Brainstorm with your colleagues, managers, subordinates, and people from other groups within your company. Aside from being a good group work practice, having other people mention your name can help open new doors. Finally, if you work for a good manager, don't be afraid to fail by trying something new.

When things are slow for you personally, get involved with something else. Find out who might need help fixing bugs, designing new features, or writing some code.

If you become the kind of person who exhibits flexibility and leadership, you'll likely be recognized and rewarded. You'll be promoted, offered management opportunities, or be chosen for a special kind of project or assignment.

Last Night I Programmed Myself to Dream about Your Space

I was having lunch with a friend and former colleague. She mentioned that the nature of software development in her company seemed to be changing. Whereas she used to design and code on her own, lately she was designing for folks overseas to code. It was also her opinion that this was going to continue and spread throughout the industry.

There are positives and negatives to this. If you really like to write code, this trend does not bode well for your future job enjoyment. However, you may like the idea that you can come up with the design of a system in the morning while busy beavers are coding it up overnight. If only it were that simple, it might be appealing. Unfortunately, unless you're very explicit, clear, and lucky, the folks who do the coding are going to have *lots* of questions. And they'll all be sitting in your email Inbox in the morning. And another day will be wasted while they await your answers before they can get back to writing your code.

No matter how you feel about this trend, it may well happen to you anyway. It pays to devote some time to studying and improving your software design skills. Get a good book on design patterns, learn UML, get good at doing rapid prototypes, and convince yourself that you really like doing more high-level work. If this doesn't happen to you, then you're no worse off. You'll get to do the coding yourself and you'll be a better designer in the end.

Job or Career?

One thing you'll need to ask yourself throughout your working life is, "Is this a job or a career?" Now, there are two definitions of the word "job". Definition one is that a job is something you show up for at 9AM, do your work, and leave at 5PM. You don't really care too much about the company (other than will they still be able to pay you next week) or what you are doing there. Definition two is that a job is a place where you work as part of your career.

A career is something that you can shape or allow to be molded. You show up at your company and are ready to invest some of yourself in it. You'll feel happy when there are successes and sad at the failures. You'll want to know where you fit in, where you don't, and how you can help.

I'm an advocate for a career with good jobs that fall under the second definition. Investing yourself in your work and your company will cause joys and sorrows, but it's the only way to live. After you've done it for a while, you may feel differently and decide that nine to five really does work better for you.

In the end, life is about the connections you make and the satisfaction you get. You can choose to get more money by hopping from company to company working on this project and that, finally getting to a high level within the company. You may be able to have great influence on what happens in your new positions and that's great, too. The most important thing with either way you choose to go is that there's more satisfaction in work that's done than a job title with nothing to show for it. No matter what path you choose, your memories and satisfaction will be better when you can remember the things you've built or helped to build.

Discussion and Thought Questions

1. Do you have any goals for your career? Do you want to be a lead software engineer, a manager, a specialist?

2. Are there projects that you can work on that might help you attain your goals?

3. Is it time to look for another place to work? Have you gotten everything that you can from your current employer?

Chapter 17: Dear Abby – Best Personal Advice

Dear Abby, Dear Abby ...
My feet are too long
My hair's falling out and my rights are all wrong

- a line from the John Prine song "Dear Abby."

Let's pretend we're just sitting down over coffee or lunch. You tell me that you're not sure where your career is going and you ask my advice about it. Here are some of the things I'd tell you. You can take it or leave it. If you find it helpful, that's great. If not, that's fine too.

Google Who?

What's so good about working for a company like Google? Well, the benefits are great. They have so much money coming in and not enough people to spread it around to. They seem like they're at the top of the heap right now. In the 70's and 80's, IBM was *the* place to work. A few years ago, Netscape and Yahoo! were all the rage. It's important to remember that places change over time and what's cutting-edge now may be old hat in a few years.

In the software industry fortunes come and go faster than you can say "pets dot com." Everyone's technology seems great when it first comes out. Money is spread around and you feel like you're on top of the world working for someone like that. Remember, however, that there's more to life than money and just working for the hottest company at the time. Many companies in this world are great places to work. You have to decide if you'd like to be small cog in a big machine, a big fish in a small pond, or a different analogy that fits somewhere in between.

Every place has the potential to compete with the Googles of the world as far as being a great place to work. Read on for how to make this happen and for how to make it feel like you're working for a company like that.

Attention, Inflated Ego in Aisle Five

This goes without saying, but there's always someone smarter than you, faster than you, stronger than you, prettier than you… No matter how well things are going for you right now, you can hit the skids in no time at all. The key to avoiding this is to avoid complacency and keep going strong.

At the Autofact conference in Detroit in 1987, Whistler Systems had a booth right next to another new company called TPC that had a brand new product that they were unveiling at the show. It was very cool and was getting a lot of buzz. Whistler's head marketing guy was ironing out a deal to do some work between the two companies as they had some complementary technology.

The most amazing thing beyond TPC's cool application was their incredible arrogance. Talking to a couple of their engineers, one of them said, in the snottiest voice you can imagine, "Yup, you guys are making a good move working with us." That guy was so stuck up you couldn't pull a needle out of his butt. Unfortunately, this corporate attitude was pervasive and even their customers ended up hating them and this hindered their sales. Eventually, other companies matched their technology and they lost their advantage.

Few things can make you more hated than having a monster ego. You want to get somewhere? Stay humble, stay hungry, and keep up the good work that got you the big head in the first place. Then, lose the big head.

Minerva, Goddess of Wisdom

Since the dawn of Computer Science, it has been a habit to make up code names, machine names, release names, or project names that sound highly intelligent. This usually manifests itself in the use of Greek or Roman gods. Perform a Google search for "Athena computer project" and you'll get

76,000 hits. Substitute Apollo and you'll get 169,000. Of course, they're not all project code names, but you get the drift. Other times, you'll see planets, their moons, or something equally important sounding used. You should resist this temptation – no one will be fooled. If you want to use something for a code name, pick something fun instead. Let everyone pick his or her favorite band for their machine name. Pick a national park for a release name. It will sound nice and evocative without trying to sound so darn smart.

So what's the compelling reason to avoid them? More experienced people have already heard them a thousand times (or 169,000 times) and they just sound amateurish. You can enhance your personal marketing or your group's by choosing something unique and creative.

American, Idle

Take a break now and then. At lunch time, go eat lunch. Get away from your desk for a while. It will refresh your head and let your creative side breathe for a minute. One thing you may find is that when you're staring at a computer, you feel pressured to type something. Unfortunately, especially when you're stuck on a problem, the one thing you need to do is think and sometimes, the worst place to find a creative solution is at your desk. Wander the halls, take a walk, go home – just get away. How many times have you thought of the answer to yesterday's problem in the shower the next morning? Let your subconscious do a little work for you.

My wife hates when I do that.

Mmmm, Magnolias

Few things are worth sacrificing your life. Fighting for your country, saving a baby from a burning building, or other heroic feats of bravery are not included in the previous statement. Specifically, this refers to work. Since I started working, I've always had outside interests. I've been practicing Judo since I was a teenager and I'm not about to stop until I can't drag myself onto the mat. I like to spend time with my wife and my daughter. I like taking hikes in the hills around where I live. I like cooking, grilling, watching football with friends, reading, watching TV, listening to music, playing the guitar, or just driving around doing errands with the top down in my convertible. In other words, I have a life.

You should have one, too. Stop and smell the roses. Take a nice vacation to somewhere you'd like to go. Meet a nice guy or girl and get married (if it's legal for you to do so). Take up a new hobby or keep doing an old one. This can be especially hard when you're young and just starting out. Your company may offer to do whatever they can to keep you at work. They'll do your laundry, run errands, or feed you lunch and dinner. All of these things are nice benefits, but they're also designed to keep you working. If you like what you're doing and enjoy the work, that's great. However, it's still important to have a life outside of work. None of your hard work will matter if you're burned out at the old age of 28 or 30. You don't have a social life, a group of friends outside of work, or a hobby. You have nothing that's fun outside of work, but you've worked so hard that even your work isn't fun any more. Doesn't sound so great, does it? Get a life.

Laughing at Funerals

You don't really want to laugh at funerals, but a sense of humor, even in the worst of times, can be amazingly helpful. A former colleague was leaving the building after being laid-off due to his department being cut out completely. As he walked down the hall, he called out, "Dead man walking!" While you felt bad for him, you had to admire his ability to let his sense of humor try to make the situation less onerous. It goes without saying that you must not be insensitive, however. If one of his colleagues who wasn't let go had yelled out the same thing, it might have been hurtful.

Not only can a good sense of humor help you get through a tough day it can also make you a valuable team member. Have you ever noticed that some people are just fun to have on your team? They don't have to be the best programmers on the team, but they make getting work done more fun, which can make everyone more productive. Great work is done in great atmospheres.

Find Out What it Means to Me

It's called respect. By now you've read the irreverent stories about nearly everyone in a company. Although there are some people in your company who haven't earned your respect and don't deserve it, it's often wise to show them some anyway.

Most of the people within your company do deserve some respect. Don't assume that anyone's job is trivial despite what you may think. A good company has many role players and your role is just one of the dozens that it takes to make things run smoothly. It's easy sometimes to think that the quality assurance, build, or install folks aren't as important as the software developers. Does it matter? Undoubtedly, you'll run into people who know more about the company, its products, and some of the product's features than you do and you can learn a great deal from them. Find a good QA person who has been around for a while and you could find a wealth of handy information. You'll also meet some real nimrods in these positions (and in software development, too), but it's best to start out with the assumption that they know what they're doing and are there to contribute. Even the hockey pucks in your company may have some information you can use. Give everyone your best attention, information, and effort and you'll earn their respect in return.

Smile versus Smiley

There's one thing you can do to help your career that's easy and actually fun, too. I have five levels of communication used in roughly this order:

1. Speak in person

2. Pick up the phone

3. Instant Message (sometimes this is 4)

4. Send an email (sometimes this is 3)

5. Avoid at all costs

Which one you pick has an impact on the connections that you make at work. I've noticed that most software developers prefer to send emails. They'll spend a half hour describing a problem in nauseating detail in an email that covers two screens. Then the person on the other end sees this monstrosity and has to wade through it. Chances are that the other person may just ignore it for a while. Do both of you a favor and either walk over to that person's desk or pick up the phone.

While you're actually speaking, find out what they're up to as well. You'll be amazed at how much you find out is going on just by speaking to people. You'll discover new functionality going into the system, new people being hired, reorganizations, new spouses, new babies, and major decisions that your manager didn't think were important enough to pass down. You simply can't get that kind of information in the response to an email.

One thing that happens in companies all the time is a snowball effect. Something starts out as an email. It may be about a complicated topic or possibly a controversial one. It is passed around, threads start to develop, and it soon becomes a traveling tome. It's time to talk.

There is a reverse side to this, however. You don't want to become known as a time sink. When you go over to a person's desk or call them on the phone, be sensitive to the fact that they may be buried in work. If you get that sense, ask if they'd *prefer* an email, especially if the issue isn't vital. Also, some people are either busy or hard to track down. Sending an email or asking via instant message if they're free to talk can help and let them pick a time that might be better for them.

Email is both the biggest boon and the biggest bane to getting things done in the world today. Used properly for notification of what's going on or for things that have flexibility in when you receive a response, it's wonderful. It's also an incredible gift to working in different time zones. However, if you need an immediate answer and are going to be stuck on a problem, PICK UP THE DAMN PHONE!

Nowadays, instant messaging has taken a more prominent role in the workplace. It's a balance between email and speaking, due to its more interactive nature. For some things, it works great. Still, this is sometimes used as a cop-out for actually talking. Want to help your career? Learn to get over your fear or hesitation to talk.

Interestingly, managers seem to have about the same level of email overuse. Especially when something touchy or personal needs to be conveyed, there's nothing like an actual conversation.

I've made so many great connections with people that I've worked because we actually spoke. I can't recommend this enough.

You may have noticed number five on the list. There are some people in your company it's best to avoid. They waste your time, are impossible to communicate with, or may be just plain nasty. You can usually make a good connection with just about everyone you meet, but some people really are oil to your water and don't mix well.

We're In Violent Agreement

Semantics can be very difficult to cut through. I've been in numerous meetings and discussions where simple semantic disagreements made convergence on a solution difficult.

You will undoubtedly find a time when you're stuck on a particular point with someone in a discussion. Sometimes a purist will simply be unwilling to budge on terminology or they may even be using it incorrectly. Your job is to figure this out and reach convergence. You might ask them to explain their definition of the term or concept that's causing the sticking point or you may need to reframe your argument. You may find in the end that you really are in agreement with each other, but that simple communication problems were preventing you from seeing that.

2+2=5

For some reason it's possible for two people to look at the same information and come up with completely difference conclusions. With something as straightforward as arithmetic, if this happens, it's because someone simply screwed up. If you've ever tried to teach someone close to you how to do something, you know that even if one person is correct it can still cause arguments. If the topic of conversion is something more open to interpretation there will often be numerous "obvious" answers. How can two groups of people on a jury see the same evidence and come up with opposite conclusions? Unfortunately, not everything is as black and white as mathematics.

Disagreements and differences of opinion happen with Democrats and Republicans, software and quality assurance, and programmers and managers. Accept that you will not always win every argument, no matter how right you are or think you are. You'll be much happier.

The Bridge on the River Kwai

Unlike the bridge in the movie, which needed to be destroyed, you should try to maintain all of the bridges that you build in your life. If there's one thing that has become obvious over the years it's that the world is very small. If there are six degrees of separation between all the people of the world, there are only three or four in the working world. Think about it for a minute. If there are only a million software developers in the

United States, or less if you're in a smaller country, what are the odds of someone knowing someone that you know?

All of these people are both a connection to your previous workplace, but also a possible connection to your next one. They're also a possible reference for you at a company if they know someone who works there. If you've burned a bridge, however, that same person might prevent your hiring at a company if they know someone there.

Even if you loathe someone, keep those bridges intact.

She's Got a Great Personality

Do you remember when you were in high school and your friends were trying to fix you up with someone who had a crush on you? They'd say, "She's got a great personality" or "He's got a great sense of humor." It rarely worked, of course, because in high school most people are so image conscious that you couldn't dream of looking past their exterior into the deeper person. In companies, however, it's easy to fall into the same trap of looking at the surface and it isn't always the best thing for you to do.

How a company looks is not a good indication of what it's going to be like to work for them. Let's say you walk into an office and the lobby looks beautiful. The receptionist is a friendly, pretty girl or handsome guy. Your first impression is that this might be a nice place to work – it's inevitable. I remember walking into several places like that for interviews. Most of the time, these are just nice buildings that this company has leased some office space in. It's not like this company necessarily built the building it's in, although it might have. Still, it tells you nothing about the manager you'd be working for, the colleagues you'd be working with, or the corporate environment. Is the place loaded with petty politics? Is the manager a micro-manager? Do people in her group look like they enjoy working there? Is there challenging, interesting work to be done? Is the place chaotic or just lively? Does the office seem empty because everyone works at home? Will they allow you to work at home occasionally when you want or need to?

All of these things affect what your work experience will be like. If you interview somewhere, ask people about what working there is like. Ask them about the best and worst aspects of the company and their jobs. Just like when you interview someone for a job and you want to ask open-ended questions to get them talking, you want to get your prospective colleagues to talk about the company.

If you are the manager, director, vice president, or president of a group or company, you have a great impact on its personality. If you foster an environment of openness, cooperation, and teamwork, your employees will give you all they've got. If you give the impression of a workplace that feeds off the fear from your employees and makes sure that everyone there worries about covering their butts then your employees are likely to be giving you the minimum effort to keep their jobs or are looking elsewhere for a better place to work.

When BDI started to sink, a colleague, Arthur, started looking at alternatives. He got an interview at ABDC and was offered a job. Two weeks later, he left the company and wanted to come back. He had thought that he would get to work on their technology and that it was cutting edge. Once he started, however, he found that most of their C++ code was just cover classes for their FORTRAN libraries and to Arthur that spelled "old technology". On top of that, BDI was a small company where everyone knew Arthur and appreciated his talents. At ABDC he was just a new, small cog in a very large machine.

Another friend from Whistler Technology took and quit two jobs in two months because he found that he didn't like the fit very well.

Part of the corporate environment is the general tone and feel of a place. The tone of an entire company can trickle down from the highest levels. If upper management creates an environment where everyone has to cover their butts, this can make life miserable. Even a protective first-line manager may only be able to do so much to insulate the developers.

If you're interviewing somewhere, finding out what its personality is can also be hard. Sometimes you just need a job and have to take what you can get. At the very least, it's better to know what you're in for from the beginning. The only way to find out is to ask.

Pay for Play

Have you ever worked somewhere where you can't believe they actually pay you to do what you're doing? It's great to work in places like that. Creating that environment isn't that hard either. Do you know that money isn't the only thing that keeps people in their current place of employment? It's up there, but not the only or most important thing. Work culture and an overall sense of belonging, appreciation, and security are also very important. If you hear someone doing something good, give them kudos. Bonuses, raises, and other benefits are fantastic, but the things that really keep you going at work are your personal satisfaction with what you're doing, working with good colleagues who are supportive of each other, and working in a place where you feel appreciated.

Even in a rigid environment like Rocky International, where they wrote flight-quality software, it could be fun. Sure it's serious work, but that doesn't mean that *you* have to be serious all the time. Sometimes, the engineers would dream up interesting things to pop up on a cockpit instrument panel. Fortunately, they kept this stuff out of the system – you *really* don't want the QA team to find this kind of thing unless you have a very informal work environment.

This Land is My Land

Few things can help your career more than getting involved in the organization. Getting involved is more than just joining the company softball team (which is great, if you like playing softball). It's really about knowing what's going on around your company. Read the press releases that may go out on a daily basis. Sure, there's lots of marketing hype, but you can find out about what products are being released and planned, what acquisitions are taking place, who's being hired to executive positions, and major reorganizations.

In addition to knowing what's going on around your company, do your best to integrate yourself with the organization. Get involved with product planning, product design, testing, documentation, marketing, and sales, in addition to just coding. You'll be surprised at how much you'll know and how you can become the "go to" person in your group when it comes to interesting projects. If you're willing to take ownership of projects or things that others have dropped, you'll be highly regarded by your company.

Perhaps the hardest thing to do can be speaking up. There are certainly times and places when this is a spectacularly bad idea. Example:

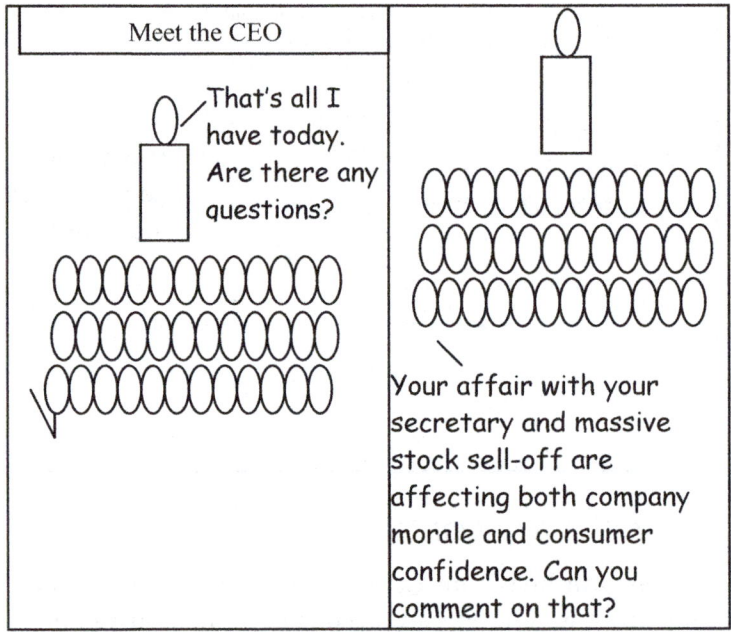

This is guaranteed to come out poorly. At huge company meetings like this, it's usually best to keep your mouth shut. The proper time to speak up is in a situation where you might really have an effect on something. In your group meeting, you might point out that a proposed solution was already tried and that it didn't work well, then propose an alternative. If you know the answer to a question, answer it. If you have a solution to a problem, say so. If you work in a place that doesn't welcome feedback, find some place that does.

Finally, there are two well-known phrases that should be kept in mind.

- The only dumb question is the one not asked.

- It is better to remain silent and be thought a fool than to speak and remove all doubt.

Knowing which one to apply at the time is crucial.

Armchair Quarterbacks

If you have the power to do it, then do it. It's easier to fix a bug when you first find it. It's easier to resolve a problem before it becomes a major sticking point. Don't procrastinate – just do it.

The cartoon above is based on a true story. Of course, there are situations where you can't just go and fix a bug due to rigid processes, but in this case, the bug sat around for months and could have just been fixed when it was first spotted.

The Night was Sultry

There will undoubtedly be times in your career when you're working nights and weekends to meet a deadline (also known as a Death March). Hopefully this will be a short-term thing and not standard operating procedure at your company. At the beginning of a more recent stint, a colleague suggested that the definition of working nights and weekends should be: "nights and weekends, but not both." This left us with some family time on the weekends at least.

If you're stuck in a situation like this, make time for your family. Pick a time of day where you can go home and spend some time with them. If you have to go back to work after eating dinner with them, at least you'll have made contact. Remember that your job may change many times during your career, but your family will hopefully be a constant, unless you neglect them.

Once Upon a Time

If you're reading this, then you've at least taken one step towards this piece of advice – read. Read a book now and then about your work. While you're waiting for the next compilation of the system you're building, pick up a book. It can be about programming in general, UML diagramming, code design, etc. Grab a magazine about business, coding, or your software's domain. Find a few good blogs about software development, like wandercoding.com. It will give you food for thought or maybe an idea that you can use on your current or future product. You never know what you might be able to use now or in the future.

That Philosophy Runs Right Through Ya

It's not often that you get to quote David Lee Roth in a book about software. In his song, "Experience", he says, "Well I'd love to talk philosophy, but I gotta take a piss. Man, that philosophy runs right through ya." There's one caveat to philosophy and experience. Philosophy without experience is crap. What? Well, if you have a personal philosophy about something, but don't have any experience with it, then it's useless.

How many times have you heard someone say, "Well, it's my philosophy that blah blah blah." You can buy that from many people, but not from someone who has no experience in actually using it. In this case, you're better off using someone else's experience and philosophy. You have people that you work with and learn from every day. Take wisdom from wherever you can get it. Try it on for a while and see if it fits you. If so, great, you can keep it. If not, try something else.

Face the Strain

Change is a difficult thing. Over time, everybody changes to some degree. Usually the changes come gradually and with some occasionally painful experiences along the way.

Sometimes in your life, you'll be asked to make changes. Some requests will be big; some small. Your husband, wife, boyfriend, girlfriend, boss, colleague, subordinate, teacher, student, or someone else will tell you something that you should change about yourself. Know this: fundamental change is very difficult. If you're being asked to change, you may feel like you can make a promise to do so without reservation, but it's just not that easy. If you're the one asking for a change in someone else, you should remember the same thing. What is easier, however, is to make small, incremental changes.

If you're asked to adopt a new process at work, adding one change at a time is easier than switching over all at once. If you're asked to improve your code quality, try adopting one strategy to add to your coding routine and then adding another, rather than fretting about all the things you might do to improve. By doing so, you can take more manageable steps and have a better chance to succeed instead of promising miracles that you're unlikely to deliver.

Fools! I'll Show You All!

In old movies, mad scientists would attempt to transplant brains from dead people to the living or other such medical miracles. When the eventual villain was ridiculed by the rest of the scientific community for his crazy scheme, he was seen being escorted out of the huge lecture hall screaming, "Fools! I'll show you all!" Well, at least that's the way the old movies are portrayed in comics and Bugs Bunny cartoons, just work with me here.

It's tempting to think that when you leave someplace after being an integral part of the organization that the place will soon fall apart. It's only natural to believe that for months on end the people will wander the halls trying to figure out how to do what you did and rue the day that you packed up and left. Unfortunately, it just doesn't happen that way. Organizations are fairly self-healing. The other people you worked with are often not the idiots you might have thought they were. You may have had a great impact on the place, but the recognition of that fact may simply get lost over time. The simple fact of life is that life goes on. Your former employer may have trouble with things in the future, but not attribute it to your absence. Perhaps you have a knack for foreseeing potential crises and helped avert several at your last job. What happened after you left? Most likely, they had the crisis and had to scramble to deal with it. Does that mean that they'll remember that you wouldn't have let it happen in the first place? Would they attribute their missed schedules to your departure? Probably not.

Unfortunately, people don't often make those connections. Some do, of course, but as a whole, organizations have short memories. That's why you see them going down the same paths, heading for the same disasters all the time. What can you do about it? Well, nothing really. What's the point after all? In your exit interview, you might politely point out all of the good things you've done for the organization in case you might want to go back to work there. The two phrases "Don't burn your bridges" and "The grass is always greener on the other side of the tracks" come into play when you leave someplace. If you leave and you're truly missed, then you've left a legacy and that's something to be proud of. If they don't miss you, that's par for the course, unfortunately.

Discussion and Thought Questions

1. Do you hesitate to speak to people? Do you think you'll bother them and decide to send an email anyway? If you're a manager, do you use email when a conversation would get the job done more quickly and efficiently?

2. Do you wish you were working for a certain company or a different company? Why or why not?

3. Do you have a life outside of work? Do you want to?

Chapter 18: Are We There Yet? – Final Thoughts

If you want a happy ending, that depends, of course, on where you stop your story.

- Orson Welles

History repeats itself because either people don't read about it in the first place, or they do, but don't recognize the parallels. Not everything you'll experience has been identically outlined somewhere in these pages, but if you look hard enough, at least some of them have. There are stories about things done well and done poorly. When you run into something, see if there's a better way to handle it than the "poor" examples or if you're headed down a worse path than the "good" story included here.

Your value in your company comes not just from what you actually program, but in the total contribution you make. Working across the boundaries of your tasks, seeing the big picture, designing functionality, designing code, solving problems, and foreseeing issues all have a great impact on your company. Being willing to help out in many capacities can go a long way in enhancing your software career. Don't be afraid to tactfully stick your nose into areas you might not be directly assigned – just know when to back off or know when you're really not wanted there.

Like people on a sports team, the most valuable player is often the one who does more than is expected or is minimally required. He's the running back on a football team who can catch passes and block well, too. She's the spiker on the volleyball team that's willing and able to dive to the floor to prevent a point. In software, if you're willing to write the code, work with your colleagues to integrate it, help to test it, know how to build it, can write some documentation, will work with the marketing and sales people, and help train people, you are worth a lot to your team.

You have many choices to make. Do you want to go into or stay in management? What kind of company do you want to work for – large, small, privately owned, publicly traded, financial, engineering, etc.? What kind of work do you want to do? Do you want to work on the internals of desktop application, the server side of a website, or the user interface of a web client? Do you want to write software that's used only within a company where you get to know the users or for an application that thousands of customers will use that you'll never meet?

If you're a manager, what kind of manager do you want to be? What kind of manager are you? Are you the "ball-buster" type who rides people to get the most out of them? Are you the "battle general" type who leads your team into combat? Are you the "mentoring and mellow" type who inspires people to work for you because they like and respect you?

Some of your decisions will likely be based on opportunities. For example, you can't work for a financial company if they won't offer you a job. Throughout my career, I've been able to find interesting work and interesting companies. I've deliberately gone after some opportunities, let the wind take me to some, and just lucked into others. Unless you're already sixty years old, you probably have a long career ahead of you. Take a chance now and then. Explore something different like a new field for you to write software in. Sometimes a different domain can make writing the same foundations of a software project more interesting. Take opportunities to learn something new like a different programming language or new technology. Keeping yourself interested and your skills fresh and varied can give you a clue in solving a problem or an advantage in getting a new job.

Finally, learn to work with all of the different people in your company. This includes the sales and marketing folks. Learning how they work and what they're after can make a big difference in how you work.

Finally, finally, visit me online at www.wandercoding.com. There you'll find more career-oriented information, my blog, and any errata that may turn up over time.

Have fun and have a great life.

Bibliography

Brooks, Herbert. 1995. *The Mythical Man Month.* Reading, Massachusetts: Addison-Wesley Professional.

DeMarco, Tom and Timothy Lister. 1999. *Peopleware.* New York, New York: Dorset House.

McConnell, Steve. 1996. *Rapid Development.* Redmond, Washington: Microsoft Press.

Spolsky, Joel. 2004. *Joel On Software.* Berkeley, California: Apress.

Index

Made in the USA
Monee, IL
07 July 2026

56550051R00136